THE COMPLETE BOOK OF
DOG BREEDING

Dan Rice, D.V.M.

BARRON'S

About the Author

Dr. Rice is a veterinarian who spent his professional career practicing companion animal medicine in Colorado. He and his wife retired to Sun City, Arizona where he now pursues his lifelong writing avocation. His recent book, *Bengal Cats,* was published by Barron's Educational Series in 1995. His freelance articles appear in local journals and magazines, and he hopes to see a volume or two of his short stories published in the near future.

All inquiries should be addressed to:
Barron's Educational Series, Inc.
250 Wireless Boulevard
Hauppauge, New York 11788

International Standard Book No. 0-8120-9604-5

Library of Congress Catalog Card No. 95-51398

Library of Congress Cataloging-in-Publication Data
Rice, Dan, 1933–
    The complete book of dog breeding / Dan Rice.
        p.   cm.
    Includes bibliographical references (p.) and index.
    ISBN 0-8120-9604-5
    1. Dogs—Breeding. I. Title.
SF427.2.R53   1996
636.7'082—dc20   95-51398
                                                        CIP

Printed in Hong Kong

987654321

Acknowledgments and Dedication

This volume is dedicated to my best friend and former partner of many years, George Dewell, D.V.M. Without his support and encouragement I could never have taken the time to work with dog breeders and fanciers, continuing my practical education in canine reproduction throughout my practice life. He also assisted me with resource material and advised on ethical points.

I wish to express gratitude to my editor, good friend, and patient advisor Mary Falcon and to Fredric Frye, D.V.M., M.S. who served as a tough (but fair) technical and literary evaluator of this work.

The American Veterinary Medical Association, American Kennel Club, and American Humane Association provided data and information included in the book. Thanks to them and to my many dog breeder friends and clients who made my life interesting over the years.

Photo Credits
Barbara Augello: front, inside front, inside back, and back covers, pages 15, 16, 45, 89, 126; Edith Varga Buchko: page 132; Eugene Butenas and Larry Naples (LCA Photography): pages 22 (left and right), 23 (left and right); Michele Earle-Bridges: page 154 bottom; Susan Green: pages 14, 68, 81, 96, 121, 152 (top and bottom), 153 (top and bottom); Paul Luna: page 29; James Pitrone (The Seeing Eye): page 66; Bob Schwartz: pages 8, 9, 19 (top and bottom), 46, 90, 104, 106, 110, 112, 116, 118, 128, 140, 154 (top), 155; Sherry Smith: pages 54, 55; Christine Steimer: pages 38, 73; Judith Strom: pages 40, 58, 60, 70, 97, 139; Toni Tucker: pages 135, 160; Wim van Vught: pages 10, 31, 85; Jean Wentworth: page 64.

Cover Photos
Front: dalmatian dam and nursing pups (Dynasty Dalmatians); inside front: doberman pinscher (Ravenswood); inside back: cocker spaniel (Snowy River); back: Labrador retriever pups (Dogwood Labs).

Important Note
Always use caution and common sense whenever handling a dog, especially one that may be ill or injured. Employ proper restraint devices as necessary. In addition, if the information and procedures contained in this book differ in any way from your veterinarian's recommendations concerning your pet's health care, please consult him/her prior to their implementation. Finally, because each individual pet is unique, always consult your veterinarian before administering any type of treatment or medication to your pet.

Contents

Chapter 1

Introduction

The goal of this book is to provide practical, usable information. It explains, defines, describes, and offers guidelines. It is not an academic text, but a handbook—a how-to book. The information contained herein is gleaned from a lifetime of personal involvement with dogs and dog breeding. The most current veterinary literature on the subject was reviewed as this book was written. This volume, written in nontechnical language, covers all aspects of breeding and raising dogs.

By definition, a *breeder* is "one who is engaged in the breeding or propagation of a specific organism." This book is intended to inform and assist four different groups of people, described below, all of whom may be considered dog breeders or potential dog breeders.

Note: Webster's dictionary defines "bitch" as a female dog. It is so used throughout this book as generally accepted canine terminology. Don't be offended by it. Also, graphic details of all aspects of canine reproduction are discussed, including the breeding act, male and female genitalia, parturition, cesarean sections, and other similar topics.

- **Experienced, established dog breeders** will benefit from reading this book. It will update their knowledge and provide new ideas and concepts. Breeding soundness examinations are covered to remind you of proven, fundamental ideas and techniques that may have fallen into disuse. Professional dog breeders, kennel operators, dog handlers, and trainers will all benefit from the information contained herein. Those of you who produce and sell puppies should consider sending a copy of this book with each puppy raised and sold. It covers the benefits of spaying and neutering, puppy and adult diseases, and vaccinations.
- **Novice dog breeders** will find a wealth of information about breeding animal selection and how and when to breed them. You will acquire important knowledge about canine estrous cycles, infertility problems, and natural and assisted breeding as well as normal whelping, dystocia emergencies and how to handle them, and the care of newborn puppies. A special section is devoted to raising orphan puppies. Sections of the book cover nutrition of the

brood bitch before breeding, during breeding, while nursing, and when weaning puppies. Puppy nutrition and how to start them on solid food is also discussed. Other sections explain pre-breeding examinations, vaccinations, general health of breeding animals, health emergencies, and medical problems associated with dog breeding.

- **Dog owners with accidentally or unintentionally bred dogs** will find this volume invaluable. You may be one of those (sometimes frantic) readers looking for help in caring for your family pet who capriciously entertained a suitor one moonlit night. These pages are filled with information relative to pregnancy determination and termination. Risks and benefits are weighed, and guidelines are established for making informed, appropriate decisions. You will discover how to make the best of an accidental and perhaps undesirable situation.

- **Potential dog breeders and dog lovers of the world** who are not presently involved with dog breeding—even those of you who don't own dogs—will find interest in this book. Perhaps you are considering purchasing a dog, and want information about breeding. Or maybe you are planning to purchase a show dog and want to know more about raising puppies. This book will satisfy the academic and practical curiosity of all those who are interested in breeding dogs.

Pet Stewardship

Whether you subscribe to the theory of evolution or the biblical account of creation, there can be little doubt that vegetation preceded animals on earth, and that the animal kingdom predated humankind. Humans depend upon the earth's plant and animal populations to supply many of their basic, life-sustaining needs. To live in unison with plants and animals, we humans accepted our mandate to steward them. We learned to use them, protect them, and control them.

Animal husbandry is among the oldest professions in the world. Management of animals has always been, and continues to be, of great concern to all cultures in every country. Animals, including birds and fish,

Indiscriminate dog breeding keeps the pounds and shelters full.

are vital resources for human beings. The protection and judicious use of those resources have long been studied and practiced by mankind.

When we think of our responsibility to manage or steward the world's animals, our first thoughts might be of domesticated meat, milk, wool, and leather-producing animals. If conservation minded, we might also reflect on the many threatened and endangered wild species. Those are certainly very serious considerations for all of us, but of equal importance is the stewardship of our pets.

Our population becomes more urbanized every year. When you contemplate the number of pets in the Unites States, it is obvious that conscientious animal husbandry must be practiced by city inhabitants as well as ranchers and wildlife organizations. Urbanites play an important part in stewardship of the world's animals!

Overpopulation

The American Veterinary Medical Association estimated the U.S. dog population in 1991 to be 52.5 million, living in 34.6 million American households.

Accurate numbers of dogs euthanized (put to sleep) annually are not available, but according to the last shelter survey, between five and ten million shelter dogs were euthanized in 1988. Hundreds of thousands of other abandoned and unwanted dogs are reluctantly destroyed by veterinarians and private citizens each year. The numbers are overwhelming! The thought of arbitrarily killing millions of helpless, harmless, loving pets brings tears of anguish and roars of indignation to our country's animal-loving population. Who can change those horrible statistics? You and I.

How can we change them? By applying wisdom we all possess, specifically, by exercising common sense in our management of pets.

Reasons for Breeding

Most dogs should be neutered before they reach breeding age. Only a select few should be bred, and then only when the breeder accepts responsibility for placing the offspring into carefully selected, loving homes where they will be properly cared for. Unfortunately, most dogs euthanized are adults. Some people love furry little pups, but fail to establish long-term relationships, and are anxious to be rid of them when they reach adulthood. That is especially true in large breeds.

Miracle of Birth

The poorest reason I ever heard for breeding a pet bitch was "to give the children firsthand knowledge of the miracle of birth." In fact, more information can be obtained from videos and books that offer professional explanations of the process. The limited impression of a few moments of reproductive education obtained by watching the birth of a puppy is not likely to earn a lofty place in a child's memory bank.

Economics

As most conscientious professional dog breeders will affirm, there's not much profit in producing top-quality puppies. Even popular purebred puppies, produced from carefully selected parents, are often difficult to place in appropriate homes. Producing healthy, strong puppies, whether purebred or mongrel, is expensive business. The necessary investment in food, health care, including vaccinations, and time is rarely recovered. As a full-time business, purebred dog breeding might show a modest profit, but as a hobby or sideline, it rarely does.

Dog Shows

Breeding purebred dogs can't be separated from showing your breeding stock. Exhibiting and competing in contests of many varieties, such as weight pulling, tracking, obedience, and conformation classes are among the greatest ways to share your time with your pet. Those exhibitions and competitions are intended to showcase the finest characteristics of dogdom. The winners exemplify the best of the best. Dog shows, obedience trials, field trials, and other competitions are the best possible places to see the finest dogs of dozens of different breeds, but dog showing is expensive! The cost of exhibition of potential breeding stock is a necessary overhead expenditure that conscientious dog breeders must accept.

Learning about Dog Breeding

Dog breeding is a very gratifying occupation if we study the breed of choice, make our breeding stock selections carefully, and apply good management techniques to our breeding program. Before beginning, we should learn as much as we can about the breeding process and raising puppies. As we study our particular breeds of dogs and what makes them great, we must also study the specifics of canine reproduction.

This book was designed to walk you through the many phases of breeding dogs in a generic way. We mention a few specific breeds as they relate to breeding or whelping problems, but our purpose is to educate you in every aspect of dog breeding, regardless of the breed you choose.

We have an ulterior motive as well. Sometimes, in spite of your best intentions, you find yourself with a pregnant bitch. She may be an expensive purebred, or a shopping basket give-away mongrel, but she is a well-loved member of your family. Quite by accident, your female puppy suddenly became a mature young lady who spent an adventuresome half hour romping in the park with some canine friends. A few weeks later it becomes obvious that she is in a "family way." After consulting with a veterinarian (see Pregnancy Termination, page 70), you decide to accept the responsibility of raising a litter of unwanted puppies.

This book was also written for you. It discusses the prediction of whelping time, normal deliveries, whelping problems, and emergencies. Whelping assistance techniques are described. You are told when to observe, when to intervene, how to help solve a problem, and when to call professional help.

Packs of stray dogs perpetuate canine health problems and overpopulation.

Owner Responsibility

No matter whether you are a professional dog breeder, a novice, a potential breeder, or a pet owner who is unintentionally thrown into the dog breeder class due to the indiscretion of your female dog, you must accept the responsibility to care for your dog and her offspring to the very best of your ability.

After accepting that precept, I offer you many years of practical experience and knowledge on the following pages.

Chapter 2
When to Breed

Seasonality of Heats

Canine reproductive biology is somewhat unique. The bitch is monestrous (having one estrus period each season), showing no seasonality of estrous cycles in most breeds. Unlike some wild carnivores, environmental temperature and climatic changes have little or no effect on domestic canine estrous. They may start their first heat period at any time of the year, whether kept in your home, outside, or in a kennel.

It is generally accepted among breeders and canine reproductive specialists that the preferred time to breed a bitch is two days after ovulation. As you will see, calculating that time in an individual bitch is not quite as easy as making the generalization.

Possible Breeding Times

Bitches can be bred during any normal heat cycle, including their first. It is a generally accepted precept that first-heat breeding is a poor practice, but sometimes it happens in spite of our good intentions. The best rule to follow when intentionally breeding a bitch is to be sure she is physically mature and mentally stable. That means she is over a year old, and depending on the breed, perhaps closer to two years, by which time she should be in her second or third heat period.

Most professional dog breeders do not include animals in their breeding program until they prove their superior qualities in bench shows or obedience competition. Working and hunting breeds likewise are rarely bred before they compete and win in the field. Certainly the overpopulation of dogs demands that we intentionally breed only those animals that are excellent representatives of the breed.

Estrous Cycle

Please note that two very similar words are used frequently in this book. The word spelled with an "o" (estr<u>o</u>us) refers to females' reproductive cycles. It includes all reproductive phases of intact (unspayed) bitches' lives. Another word that is pronounced identically (estrus) is spelled without an "o," and refers to "standing heat" periods, which are the second specific phases of estrous cycles. It is important to understand the differentiation. I will endeavor to use estrous only in combination with the word "cycle."

Phases of the Estrous Cycle

Canine heat cycles are divided into four separate phases. Each phase has specific outward signs associated with it, as well as attitude, hormonal, and other internal changes. The paragraphs discussing hormone changes may seem academic, but if read carefully, you will find the information fascinating. The hormone discussion allows one to more fully understand the attitude and appearance changes of the bitches as they progress through their estrous cycles.

Blood serum hormone levels can best be determined by laboratory analysis using a technique called radioimmunoassay (RIA). Other techniques are adapted for home use. The home ELISA (enzyme-linked immunoabsorbent assay) test for progesterone is less accurate, but often valuable if interpreted correctly.

Proestrus

The first estrous cycle phase is called *proestrus*. Its outward, physical signs are obvious. All the female's reproductive tissues thicken, her vulva swells, and visi-

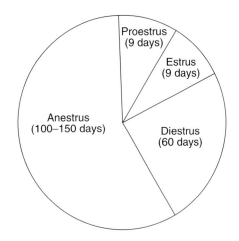

Chart illustrating phases of estrus cycle of a bitch, using average data.

ble genitalia becomes reddened. Bloody vaginal discharges are produced, and the bitch usually spends an extraordinary amount of time licking her external genitalia. She may act nervous and her appetite is reduced. In early proestrus, some bitches are snappy toward other animals.

As the days of proestrus count down, she tries to escape from confinement, seeking a mate. The bloody discharge attracts males from near and far. If housed with intact males, they will begin paying court to the bitches. If females are allowed outside, male dog visitors should be expected.

Prior to puberty, intact bitches' internal reproductive organs (except their ovaries) are quite undeveloped. The actual weight and dimensions of prepuberal (before the first heat) uteruses are significantly smaller than those of sexually mature animals. As puberty is reached and proestrus begins, the uterus enlarges in response to hormones secreted from the ovaries. Although that enlargement is unapparent to the owner, it can sometimes be palpated by veterinarians with practiced fingers, and it is easily demonstrated by ultrasound imaging.

Proestrus lasts from two to 27 days, more typically seven to ten days. The average length of proestrus is generally accepted to be nine days.

During this phase, estrogen hormone levels rise gradually in the bloodstream, and levels of the progesterone hormone remain relatively low.

Another hormone called *follicle stimulating hormone* (FSH) originates from the pituitary gland. For two or three weeks prior to the onset of proestrus, serum levels of FSH rise. Its effect is to stimulate production of follicles within the ovaries. These follicles contain microscopic eggs called *ova*.

Estrus

The next phase of the reproductive cycle is termed *estrus*. It corresponds to the stage often referred to as "standing heat," when bitches will stand for breeding. It lasts from extremes of two to 21 days, more typically six to ten days, and averages nine days. It is during estrus that a bitch will mate with a male; spontaneous ovulation takes place during this phase.

Beautifully conditioned boxer feeding her plump, aggressive puppies.

Variations in females' standing heat behavior may be due to hormonal changes in progesterone-estrogen ratios. Another equally important consideration that all breeders must acknowledge is female discretion. Studies have repeatedly shown that females' breeding behavior can sometimes be changed simply by changing available mates (see Chapter 4 for more on this subject).

A vaginal discharge normally persists throughout the estrus period, but it changes from the bloody red of proestrus to a light pink or straw color as ovulation time nears. During estrus, most bitches will flirt with males by backing up to them, flagging their tails in the males' faces, urinating frequently, and generally acting seductive. Females will sometimes mount available males and simulate copulation.

Estrogen hormone levels remain about the same, and progesterone levels begin to rise during estrus. Bitches become receptive to males as a result of interaction between estrogen and progesterone. Standing heat lasts several days, sometimes a week. After the first day on which a bitch will receive a male, estrogen levels drop and progesterone levels increase greatly.

Another measurable hormone should be mentioned. It is called *lutenizing hormone* (LH) and it originates from the pituitary gland. LH levels peak in the female's bloodstream at the time she will first

Three healthy King Charles spaniel puppies at the dinner table.

stand for a male. It has been determined that ovulation (release of eggs from ovarian follicles) occurs one to three days after the LH peak. In certain problem breeders, this information is of critical importance (see Chapter 4, Potential Breeding Problems).

Ovulation

Of further importance and interest is the time of ovulation and its relationship to fertilization of the ova (eggs). According to research published by Sokoloweski in 1977, there are about 700,000 ova present in a bitch's ovaries prior to puberty (see References, page 169). By the time of her second or third heat, a quarter of a million remain. A rather large number of these eggs are expelled from ovarian follicles during each estrus. That expulsion of ova from her ovaries is called *ovulation*.

Nervous beagle dam standing on leash to allow her energetic pups to nurse.

about six days after the LH peak. It takes place in the oviducts, and one sperm cell unites with a single ovum. Normal, healthy males' ejaculates contain enormous numbers of viable sperm. Ovaries may produce dozens of ova, of which usually less than 20 are fertilized and remain viable. The number of embryos that survive, implant in the uterus, and grow to become puppies is only a tiny fraction of the potential.

Embryonic Implantation

Puppies' lives begin on the road as the microscopic embryos travel along the oviducts and into the horns of the uterus over a period of eight to 12 days after breeding. Embryos finally implant (attach) in the highly vascular wall of the uterus about 17 or 18 days after mating. The number of embryos attached in each horn is not necessarily equal. In cesarean sections I commonly found one uterine horn to contain only one fetus or sometimes none, and half a dozen or more fetuses in the other. This has no known significance, and is mentioned only as a point of interest. Embryos do not normally attach in the body of the uterus.

Breeding Time

Since ovulation takes place a day or two after the bitch will first accept a male, it seems likely that a breeding program will be highly effective if we breed a bitch as soon as she will receive a male,

Ovulation is spontaneous in the bitch; all mature ovarian follicles rupture at the same time, releasing their ova into the fallopian tubes (oviducts) that lead from the ovaries to the uterus. After releasing its eggs, each ruptured follicle shrinks and is thereafter called a *corpus luteum* (yellow-body). Unruptured follicles return to inactivity until the next estrus period.

Ova have a fertile life span of one to four days. If a bitch is bred, the actively swimming sperm find their way from where they are deposited in the vagina through the cervix, into and through the length of the uterus, and into the oviducts. Canine sperm cells have a vital life of about seven days.

Actual fertilization, that is the union of sperm and ova, occurs

then repeat the breeding two days later. Generally, conception is more likely following the earliest possible normal breeding.

Be skeptical of literature or old wives' tales about breeding on specific days of the estrous cycle. Forced breeding or artificial insemination of a bitch on an arbitrarily assigned day may be doomed to failure. Conception success depends not on what is written, but on a bitch's attitude, her general health, and how well her hormones are working. Most of us who have kept intact females can attest to the fact that when "turned out," most bitches do quite well on their own. Nature's timing seems to be highly effective.

While males are usually indiscriminate in their choice of mates, many times females will select their partners with discretion, allowing only a particular male or two the privilege of mating with her. Unfortunately, they do not always make the most prudent choices when left to their own devices.

Puppies of a single litter may be sired by more than one male. That usually occurs if the bitch is allowed to cruise the streets to choose her own mate(s), and is bred by several males during her receptive period (a practice to be discouraged at all costs).

Artificially Induced Estrus

Using female hormones, it is fairly simple to chemically induce outward signs of normal estrus in

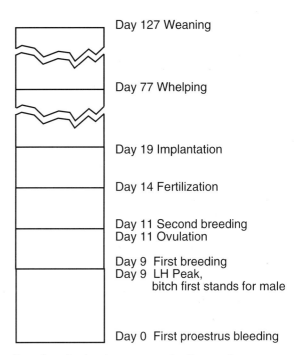

Day 127 Weaning

Day 77 Whelping

Day 19 Implantation

Day 14 Fertilization

Day 11 Second breeding
Day 11 Ovulation

Day 9 First breeding
Day 9 LH Peak,
        bitch first stands for male

Day 0 First proestrus bleeding

Breeding chart, using averages for the species.

bitches. Artificially producing a fertile estrus is quite another project. A great many research trials conducted over several decades have yielded inconclusive results. Some trials reported relatively consistent success using oral estrogens daily. Some of that work is difficult or impossible to reproduce in practice.

Other researchers in the past had relatively good and reproducible success using a series of injections of estrogens, lutenizing hormone (LH), and follicle stimulating hormone (FSH). Unfortunately, LH hormone is no longer commercially available.

Diestrus
(Formerly Called Metestrus)

The third stage of canine reproductive cycles is known as diestrus. In literature from prior years, this phase was called *metestrus*, and had a slightly different academic definition. For practical purposes, metestrus and diestrus are synonymous. Diestrus lasts about 60 days. It is currently defined as the period extending from the last day a bitch will accept a male until the termination of pregnancy. If she is not mated, a female's outward appearance during diestrus is indistinguishable from anestrus (see below).

Because ovulation is spontaneous in the bitch, it is not signified by outward signs, receptivity, or male interest. Once ovulation occurs, the follicles from which eggs were discharged begin to recede. Diestrus is under the influence of the hormone progesterone, which originates from those corpora lutea (plural of corpus luteum). Progesterone is often called the hormone of pregnancy, and is responsible for the maintenance of the uterus and the fetuses implanted and growing therein.

Anestrus

For about 100 to 150 days, bitches' reproductive systems are in a quiet stage of the estrous cycle known as anestrus. One reference lists the anestrus period as two to nine months. As in other phases of the cycle, breed, condition, nutrition, and size influence the duration of anestrus. During that period, bitches exhibit no signs of heat. Their external genitalia (vulvas) remain normal in size and color, and there is no vaginal discharge. Their temperaments and dispositions are normal, and they show no sexual interest in males. It is the period of uterine rest, repair, and stabilization.

The only reproductive hormone found in the bloodstream in appreciable quantities during anestrus is estrogen. Although some consider anestrus to be a period of reproductive inactivity, the animal's pituitary gland and ovaries are actively preparing for the next proestrus phase to begin.

As you can see, proestrus accounts for about nine days, and estrus for another nine; diestrus accounts for two months, and anestrus four or more months. Most bitches (except basenjis) complete more or less two estrus cycles each year. The age at which cycles commence depend less on climatic conditions and geographical variations, and are more influenced by nutrition, health, and physical size.

Interestrous Period

The time interval between periods of receptivity of canine females is termed the interestrous period. It varies greatly between breeds and between individuals within a breed. One lengthy study found the interestrous interval in German shepherds to be as short as 149 days, and in Boston terriers to be as long as 242 days. Bassets, beagles, cockers, Pekingese, and poodles fell in between.

German shepherds and rottweilers sometimes have estrous cycles of four months or less. Bitches that demonstrate interestrous intervals of less than 130 days may not have ample organ repair and preparation time during anestrus. Infertility is occasionally seen in those animals and hormone treatment can often be used to lengthen their interestrous periods.

Age

Canine estrous or heat cycles begin at puberty and occur throughout intact bitches' lives until death. Spaying (removing the uterus and ovaries) ends the estrous cycles. Puberty is reached at varying ages—at five months in some toy breeds, or as late as 30 months in some giant breed individuals.

Many canine research studies use beagles as models. In that breed, puberty is typically reached at about ten months, and it directly correlates with growth plane maturity. Since smaller breeds mature at a younger age than large breeds, it usually follows that tiny breeds experience puberty at an earlier age than giants. If your bitch has not shown evidence of a heat period by two years of age, consult your veterinarian or a canine reproductive specialist.

We ordinarily speak of canine estrous cycles as six-month periods, but rarely do they take exactly six months to complete. The lengths of cycles not only vary between breeds, but considerable differences are common between females of the same breed. An individual bitch's cycles are usually very predictable from year to year, but they may also vary due to health and condition influences. Some authorities speculate that the duration of lactation (length of time she nurses her puppies) may modify a particular bitch's cycle as well.

Most canine females' estrous cycles occur more or less twice a year. Exceptions to that rule are found in the basenji breed and in wolf hybrids. Those animals typically exhibit only one estrous cycle per year. It is interesting to note that the age a female reaches puberty relates to her body size or growth plane, but the length of estrous cycles is not correlated to body size.

Seasonality

Dogs' fertility (the propensity for normal pregnancy) does not seem to differ in response to its climatic seasonal environment. An extensive study of a number of breeds and cross-bred dogs showed that estrus activity (periods of receptivity of females) were identical in January and July (11.4 percent in each month). A slight reduction of estrus

American Eskimo puppies preparing for action.

activity was observed in December (10.9 percent), and the rest of the months of the year saw very similar figures (6.4 to 8.3 percent). Seasonal or climatic changes seem to influence the estrous cycles of feral canine populations.

Condition

Other than body size and breed peculiarities, several other factors influence puberty and estrous cycles. Among them are injuries, diseases, nutrition, and the presence of other intact females in the same home or kennel. They are discussed at length in the chapter on breeding problems (Chapter 4).

The general health and fitness of bitches play extremely important roles in their reproductive cycles. Animals exhibiting or recovering from injuries or illnesses may not cycle, or their cycles may be abbreviated or otherwise modified. That is another general rule to which exceptions are frequently noted.

I have seen live, reasonably healthy puppies born to weak, emaciated bitches suffering from poor nutrition, complicated by infections, intestinal parasites, fleas, and ticks. High puppy mortality usually accompanies such litters, but dogs have an amazing ability to perpetuate their species in the face of adversity.

Example: I had occasion to treat a 30-pound mixed breed bitch about eight months old that a client picked up on the roadside of an Arizona Indian reservation. She was emaciated, anemic, weak, dehydrated, and nearly comatose. One femur was fractured with the bone ends overriding each other several inches. Her coat had once been long, but was now sparse due to an active mange infestation. She also harbored three types of intestinal parasites.

Together with general anesthesia and surgical bone repair, she was treated for her various parasite infestations and anemia. Her response to treatment and premium diet was exemplary. On a splint check-up visit two weeks later, I discovered she was about one month pregnant. Spaying her was considered, but her new owners elected to wait until after her other ailments were handled. Due to her stressed condition, I predicted she might not carry the litter to term. Surprise! She uneventfully delivered and raised five nondescript puppies.

Nutrition

Females with nutritional deficits due to starvation, poor quality food or unbalanced diets may cycle normally but they may not conceive when bred. Some conceive but abort or resorb (see Fetal Resorption and Abortion, page 59)

Boston terrier youngsters taking a basket break.

embryos early in gestation. The nutritional status of a bitch relates to the quantity and quality of food offered (see Pregnancy Nutrition, page 67) as well as her ability to normally absorb and metabolize the food she eats.

Parasites

Another important aspect of a dog's general condition is associated with parasite infestation. Animals that are supporting large populations of internal or external parasites are being robbed of nutrition, regardless of the quality and quantity of food consumed (see Health and Immune Status of a Female, page 28).

Obesity

Obese bitches often have erratic estrus cycles as well. Obesity may relate to simple glutinous overeating, eating a high calorie, unbalanced diet, lack of exercise, or occasionally, endocrine imbalances.

Induced Estrus (Dormitory Effect)

A unique and poorly explained canine estrous idiosyncrasy is often reported in scientific literature without interpretation. It is especially prevalent in kenneled dogs, but may also be seen when two adult, intact females live in the same house.

A bitch in heat influences other intact bitches in the immediate environment to begin proestrus. Sometimes referred to as the dormitory effect, it is studied by a few, denied by many doubters, and affirmed by most of us. Simply put, typical proestrus, followed by normal standing heat may be induced in one female by another bitch in heat. I doubt that anyone fully understands the mechanism of induced estrus, but some experts believe that it may be due to pheromones that are produced by bitches in the proestrus or estrus phase of the estrous cycle. (Pheromones are chemical substances produced by one animal that stimulate certain behavioral responses in other animals of the same species.)

Split Heats

False heats, sometimes referred to as "split heats," are phenomena that often confuse dog breeders as well as veterinarians. Females display outward signs of normal proestrus, then, before breeding times are reached, heat signs disappear. They show no signs of heat for several weeks, then begin normal proestrus followed by standing heat.

I have also heard the term "wolf heat," used in reference to split heats. The explanation referring to wild canines suggests that female wolves exhibit a few days of proestrus bleeding to signal males that breeding time is approaching. The brief prostrus signs also tend

Shiba-Inu puppy cleaning her brother's face.

to induce heat in other females, thus setting the stage for breeding male selection and general gathering of the pack for annual reproductive rites.

Maturity

A bitch's sexual maturity relates to puberty, ovulation, acceptance of a male, and conception. If a capable male is present, she will stand and can be bred for several consecutive days during the estrus stage of any normal heat.

Our discussion of the best time to breed your bitch should include more than her willingness or ability to be bred. Unfortunately, bitches that are not confined behind a dog-proof fence are sometimes mismated on their first heat. No matter how well trained she is, when left to her own devices, the influence of hormones and inherent desire to perpetuate the species take precedence over all else.

At what age should a bitch be bred? All generalities are dangerous. One often hears that no dog should be bred until her second heat, or until she is one year old. That implies all dogs mature at the same rate and by the same age. Alas, that is not the case at all. Sometimes individuals of all breeds are very immature at one year of age, and should not be bred until they are much older. Others may not reach puberty until long past one year of age. Large and giant breeds may be physically

mature by the time they experience their first heat when they are 18 or 20 months old. Toys may cycle twice by one year of age. Experts state that full sexual maturity relates to the attainment of maximum capacity for reproductive performance, and that is no sooner than the second or third estrus period.

I suggest there is yet another important factor in the equation—the owner's readiness to accept the responsibility of bringing a litter of puppies into the world.

Male Puberty

Males, like females, reach puberty at varying ages, depending on the breed. Most males of all breeds are sexually mature and capable of producing puppies by a year of age. The smaller breeds usually mature earlier than the large and giant breeds. Many litters of unscheduled, undesired puppies are the products of sexually precocious males that are physically immature.

I can recall many phone calls from distraught clients, saying, "Doctor, I need help. Who would have guessed that our neighbor's little six-month-old cockapoo-rat terrier cross was old enough to be romantically interested in my purebred Pekingese? I can't understand how he managed to get over our three feet (91 cm) high fence. Now, can you believe it? I think the ugly little rascal is somehow fastened to sweet little Ling Choy.

Surely he hasn't gotten her in a family way, has he?"

Never underestimate the virility or the persistence of a clumsy young neighborhood puppy. There is an old adage bantered among purebred dog breeders: "The uglier the mutt, the better the fence jumper."

If your beautiful, purebred show bitch is in heat and a wandering, nondescript pooch can find his way through, under, or over your fence, you may find it necessary to contact your veterinarian for a discussion of abortion techniques (see Pregnancy Termination, page 70).

Stud Dog Age

When breeding a young bitch for the first time, it is often best to use a proven stud dog. His experience will certainly help in the actual breeding process, and a secondary benefit is your ability to see and handle his offspring from previous matings. Such studs will usually be more than a year old, perhaps much older.

Males that are proven in shows or other competitions are usually also well over a year of age. The number of champions under a year of age is relatively small. In purebred dog breeding, a stud's age is secondary to his quality and the quality of puppies he has produced with other females.

Some novice purebred dog breeders are guilty of a serious mistake—they obtain male and female puppies of their chosen breed at the same time. Sometimes the pups are closely related, often littermates. Before they have the opportunity to establish their quality in the show ring, the female comes into heat. They aren't old enough for conformation shows, obedience, or field trials, but they are old enough to breed. The bitch shows signs of proestrus bleeding, and the owner leaves them together, either unwittingly or intentionally, to let nature take its course. Which it does.

The result can be a nightmare. The progeny of inbreeding between littermates or other closely related parents may exhibit exaggerated features found in their parents. Carefully planned inbreeding should be left to experts with extensive genetic knowledge of their dogs. Inbreeding may intensify physical faults that are easily recognized, or they may amplify unapparent personality traits. People shopping for pets are well advised to be suspicious of inbred puppies, which makes it difficult to place them in good homes.

Even if the pups are not related, first-season breeding is not good management technique. If it happened to you, read on; we'll help you make the best of it.

Female spaniel displays flirting attitude typical in proestrus or early estrus. Black and white male knows what to do, but is unsure when to begin.

Matched pair of black and tan cockers share kisses in quiet courting scene.

Chapter 3

Choosing and Conditioning Brood Stock

Books written about specific breeds guide the prospective buyer through breed standards and explain how to select the best possible representative of each breed. They dwell on conformation, preferred coat type, colors, size, and personality of the subject breed. This is a generic book not limited to individual breeds, but one that supplements those written about individual breeds.

One fact is found in every good dog breeding book. Cheap breeding stock is very expensive. It costs just as much to propagate average quality as it does to produce the top of the line.

In your breed selection process, you no doubt attended many dog shows and other competitions. You talked with other breeders and committed breed standards to memory. You plan to show your bitch a number of times, receiving appropriate awards, points, and ribbons. You are convinced that she possesses the potential to produce puppies that will be excellent representatives of your chosen breed.

You are aware of hereditary faults that sometimes show up in your breed, and took precautions to assure that your dog is not afflicted with any. No hereditary problems have been diagnosed in her parents or siblings.

You are financially and physically able to care for a bitch in whelp and willing to accept the responsibilities associated with delivery and raising a litter of puppies. You have formulated a plan for placing the puppies in homes where they will be loved and cared for.

Now you need advice on the specifics of breeding animal selection, such as the temperamental, nutritional, and reproductive health characteristics of a good dam and sire.

Temperament

No matter which breed you choose, regardless of how similar

they appear, all dogs of a breed are not identical. Each individual has its own genetic makeup. Its temperament as an adult reflects the dispositions of both parents as well as its bonding and treatment as a puppy. If you already own the dog that you plan to breed, it may be too late to look at its parents' temperaments, but you can still objectively analyze your dog's attitude. Your decision to breed a dog with a grouchy, snappy disposition might have horrible consequences.

Example: I knew a large male dog of a breed that is known for its aggressiveness as guards. I examined the animal in the clinic dozens of times without incident. I trimmed and sanded his toenails, treated infected ears, vaccinated him, and otherwise tested our relationship regularly. He was a pussy cat—not an aggressive bone in his body.

In his exhibition career he was shown frequently in both conformation classes and obedience trials, where his handlers and judges saw no evidence of a disposition fault. He easily acquired the points necessary to receive both his AKC conformation championship and CD obedience degree. He belonged to a family with three small children, all of whom wrestled and played with him daily.

He displayed one personality problem, and that was only manifested in his own home. When he was six or seven months old, his owners discovered he had a quick temper and was sensitive to being touched by anyone other than his family. He did not aggressively attack strangers, and he tolerated household visitors very well as long as they kept a respectable distance. When touched by them, however, his immediate response was to snap. Because he had never actually attacked or bitten anyone, his owners accepted what they considered to be a minor character quirk.

One day, when the dog was about four years old and weighed over 85 pounds, a tragedy occurred. A six-year-old girl, who lived next door and regularly visited the family, put her arm around the dog's neck as the children sat on the floor watching TV. He responded by ripping her face and ear, leaving her scarred for life.

The consequences of that incident were far reaching. They included several years of terribly painful, modestly successful but very expensive plastic surgery, a divorce, the sale of a home, and long, spiteful litigation between former friends and neighbors.

Between two and four years of age, after winning his championship in the show ring, the dog sired several litters of beautifully marked, excellent conformation puppies, many of whom displayed the same untrustworthy characteristic as adults. Consequently, at least three or four of the puppies were euthanized over the next few years.

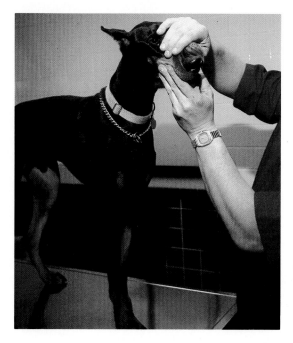

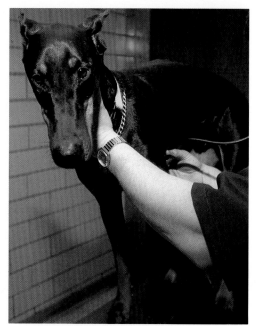

The moral of the story is simple. Personality traits are important and, to some degree, hereditary. Dams and sires must be evaluated for more than their conformity to breed standards. A conscientious breeder should select a puppy whose parents are known to have an agreeable temperament. When choosing a pup as a breeding animal, handle both its sire and dam. If possible, meet and handle dogs produced previously from both the sire and dam.

A dog breeder should always try to improve the breed. To include animals with personality faults in your breeding program is just as dangerous as including animals known to have hip dysplasia or hereditary eye problems.

Nutrition of Breeding Animals

Choosing a female to breed must include careful consideration of her condition. A brood bitch's nutrition should be an extension of her nutrition as a puppy. As a youngster she should be fed a diet that allows her physical growth and development to proceed at a regular, average rate. When she reaches adulthood, her maintenance diet, exercise, and eating habits should assure that she does not become obese, and that she displays firm musculature.

It is a mistake to try to reduce or fatten up animals at breeding time. Obesity favors erratic reproductive

behavior. Skinny, undernourished bitches may not cycle normally, and if successfully bred, the stress of pregnancy and lactation will cause further trouble.

Breeding bitches should be in lean and gaining condition when they begin their estrus cycles. Their regular maintenance diets should be increased about 5 percent when they show the first signs of proestrus bleeding. Diets are then reduced to maintenance levels following breeding, and gradually increased again one month into gestation (see Pregnancy Nutrition, page 67).

The following general nutritional comments apply equally to breeding, pregnancy, and lactation diets.

Specific recommendations relative to those reproductive phases are found in other sections of this book.

Food Storage

Don't buy excessive quantities of dry dog food at one time. Storage takes its toll on nutrients—fats may become rancid, vitamins A, D, E, K, and some B complex may be lost. Beware of buying dry dog food from stores that have low product inventory turnover.

Preservatives and additives help maintain palatability of dry foods, and will help protect them from early oxidation. In large kennel situations, when hundreds of pounds of food are purchased at one time, storage problems may be

An otoscope is used to examine outer ear canals, and the dog's weight is recorded.

All dog foods are not the same! Learn to read pet food labels before buying.

ans. Those products provide the type of nutrition that will enhance reproductive success if fed according to directions. Some premium brands formulate special diets for breeding animals during gestation and lactation. Nutritional information on the package will specify whether the product provides optimum nutrients for growth in puppies, brood bitches, lactating dams, or adult maintenance.

Dog Foods

The nutrient composition of your brood bitch's food must be known in order to evaluate its nutritional balance and caloric intake. Sometimes that information is not easily accessible.

A word of advice: If the package of dog food you are planning to feed does not plainly display its composition and ingredients, buy another food. There is sufficient competition in the dog food industry today to allow intelligent dog breeders to shop for the best quality products. Products containing the best ingredients and balanced compositions will proudly and prominently display that information.

Know what you are feeding! All dog foods are not alike. Read package labels, call, or write to manufacturers. Products are not identical simply because their fat contents are the same, or their protein levels have the same numbers. It is a serious mistake to buy dog food based on price or total protein quantity. It

even worse. Sometimes the food is subjected to high temperatures, especially on the bottom of the stack. Deterioration is enhanced by elevated temperature.

Except for quantities fed, it isn't necessary to change a bitch's diet during her reproductive cycle, providing she is in excellent nutritional condition, being fed a complete, balanced, premium quality dog food. It is an established fact that poor reproductive function is associated with marginal nutrition. Considering that your bitch has only two estrus cycles per year, if she misses the desired breeding time, the planned puppies will be at least six months late in arriving.

There are many premium foods available in pet supply stores, some supermarkets, and from veterinari-

makes no more sense than choosing the food by the picture on a bag. Be selective. Don't fall for TV ads showing a beautiful litter of puppies or a happy bitch. Those are paid actors; they are marketing tools. They might be promoting an excellent product, or one designed with the singular purpose of making money for the manufacturer. The sources of protein, carbohydrate, and fat are equally as important as the quantities. Think of ingredient quality as well as quantity.

Dog Food Labels

Some labels state that the foods meet or exceed recommendations of the NRC (National Research Council). That statement may apply only to canine maintenance requirements and may not consider the increased energy demands of breeding, pregnancy, or lactation.

Labels may specify the quantities of available nutrients, not the bioavailable nutrients. If an essential element is fed to a dog in a form that is not bioavailable (that is, the amount that is assimilated and metabolized by the animal), it might as well be left in the bag. Always look for the source of protein. The ingredient list should give you that information. Vegetable protein sources such as corn or soy flour may provide an excellent analysis on the package, but that may be misleading.

Labels stating that a food meets or exceeds requirements for growth and maintenance mean just what they say. Such products should not be fed during breeding, gestation, or lactation.

Foods labeled with statements that they meet or exceed NRC recommendations for all stages of life are what you want, right? Getting close, but still not enough. Keep looking.

Feeding Trials

You will find foods with label declarations that they have passed the *American Association of Feed Control Officials (AAFCO) feeding trials for the entire life cycle of canines*. You can generally rest assured that products so labeled contain the right amount of bioavailable food elements required by a brood bitch. If the AAFCO declaration is not shown, get the free phone number from the package and call the manufacturer. Obtain feeding trial results and ask about the source of protein and fat.

Request printed information about formulation of products, and whether the formula is kept constant, regardless of seasonal variation of ingredient costs.

If you are unable to obtain desired information about products, exercise your option to choose other brands, and if you are unable to understand information provided by manufacturers, consult with your veterinarian. If he or she isn't able to help you make an intelligent selection, borrow a text on the subject. Most veterinary clinics have numerous reference sources for nutritional requirements of dogs.

Generic Brands

Generic and house brand products sometimes contain only 15 to 22 percent protein and too little fat for a brood bitch's diet. When shopping, always consider generic brands, but before buying, be sure they conform to the standards we have discussed. Check the amounts and sources of essential elements, as well as feeding trial results.

Protein Quality

Protein of plant (vegetable) origin, such as soy, cottonseed, safflower, or corn, offers a less desirable amino acid spectrum than meat-based products. Amino acids from vegetable proteins have lower bioavailability than those from animal proteins. Relative to canine optimum nutrition, plant protein is of less quality than animal protein.

Fats

Adequate fat must be included in brood animals' diets. Fat is a calorie-dense nutrient, containing nine kcal per gram (more than twice the calories of protein and carbohydrates). This is true of both animal fat and vegetable oil. Palatability is the principal difference between vegetable oils and animal fats. Both provide adequate fatty acids.

Carbohydrates

Carbohydrates are a principal source of glucose in human food, but are much less important in canine diets. They are another source of calories derived from plants. Canine metabolism produces glucose from fat (through its glycerol), and from protein (through its amino acids). Dogs, therefore, do not depend on carbohydrates for glucose.

Starches or carbohydrates have low caloric density, and in dogs, they lack good digestibility and palatability. Although carbohydrates are not required by dogs, diets without them are impractical to produce. Diets high in carbohydrates, in which most of the protein and fat are also of plant origin, are not recommended for breeding dogs.

Types of Food

Three basic types of dog food are presently on the market. Many companies produce all three.

Canned foods are expensive, but they store well and are highly palatable.

Soft moist foods are also palatable, but do not store as well. They are also expensive and contain some questionable chemical preservatives that are not found in dry foods.

Dry foods are usually the least expensive and easiest to feed. Most premium brands are also well accepted by dogs.

Generally, premium dry dog foods contain very adequate nutrition, require no supplementation, and are sufficiently palatable to suit most finicky appetites. In many cases, especially in house-pet breeding animals, they may be fed free-choice. Naturally, that is not an option if your bitch is a glutton.

To increase palatability, a basic diet of complete and balanced dry food can be mixed with canned food that is also complete and balanced.

Supplements

It is poor economics to feed a bargain brand of dog food, hoping to cover its deficiencies with a cheap vitamin and mineral supplement. Do not arbitrarily supplement your breeding bitch's diet with vitamins or minerals. If she is established on a recommended diet, they are unnecessary. If your veterinarian has approved feeding a multiple vitamin-mineral supplement to your dogs, specifically including breeding animals, it is fine to continue to do so.

A word of caution: It is dangerous to add raw meat, bone meal, or other similar products to breeding animals' already complete, balanced diets. It is true that animal protein supplementation was widely researched and used in the past. For years, nutritionists recommended additions of meat, especially liver, to dry dog food diets of breeding animals. That was primarily due to the extensive use of corn and soy flours in the dry food formulas. Protein quality was suspect and amino acid

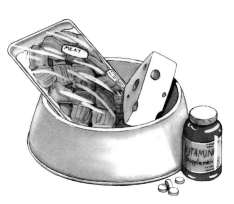

Dietary supplements are usually unnecessary and may be harmful.

deficiencies were sometimes experienced in those diets.

Today, due to extensive research by pet food manufacturers, private research foundations, and universities, we have more information about nutritional needs of our pets. Complete, balanced diets have been formulated for us. For individuals who want to delve into the specifics of dog nutrition, I recommend the book *Nutritional Requirements of Dogs, Revised*, from the National Research Council, telephone 1-800-624-6242. This volume, which is updated regularly, will answer virtually all technical questions about canine nutrition.

Home-made Diets

Diets formulated and produced in the family kitchen often lead to problems. If you are determined to cook for your dog, the above-cited book will supply information on such diets. I heartily recommend that you follow its guidelines closely. However, in my experience, it is best to leave formulation and production of dog foods to those who have laboratories, research facilities, and feeding trials to prove their products.

Health and Immune Status

Conditioning a breeding animal is not complete without consideration of its general health and vaccination history. Before your brood bitch is due to come into heat, or upon the first signs of proestrus vaginal bleeding, schedule a visit to your veterinarian. A physical examination is an excellent investment prior to breeding (see Pre-breeding Evaluation, page 44). Even in proven brood bitches that have been bred and produced puppies previously, an examination is recommended. Your health care professional may detect something minor such as an ear infection or dental problem that needs correction before the stress of breeding and pregnancy begins.

The examination will affirm your dog's nutritional and general health status, and recommendations may be made about exercise or dietary changes. A fecal (stool) sample will probably be requested to determine if she has intestinal parasites. If the test is positive, treatment will be arranged to relieve the stress of the parasites and minimize their passage to the puppies.

Heartworm protection will be discussed and recommendations about the best prevention techniques that are compatible with breeding animals.

Your veterinarian will update you on anything new on the immunization scene. He or she will probably recommend vaccinations for your bitch to assure that the highest possible immunity and disease protection will be passed to the puppies.

In the rapidly advancing animal biological and pharmaceutical industries, new products and techniques enter the arena regularly. It is not appropriate to list each parasite and its treatment in this book or to advise you about which vaccines should be administered to your brood bitch. Some diseases are prevalent in one part of the country and virtually absent in others. Biologicals that were appropriately administered to a breeding animal last year may be less effective than new vaccines that just emerged from the laboratories (see Some Diseases Preventable by Vaccinations, page 152).

Even if you treat your dogs for parasites at home, it is important to use the best products and to have the latest information. Update your knowledge through a consultation with your veterinarian, even if it is only a phone call. Ask about flea and tick collars and other insecticide products. Inquire about vermifuges (worm medications) that are safe to use during breeding, gestation, and lactation. A number of chemicals are contraindicated during bitches' reproductive phases.

It is unlikely you will see the most up-to-date information in your daily newspaper. Advertisements and package inserts are easily misinterpreted or misleading. Place your trust in information from professionals whose business it is to stay currently informed.

Selecting a Suitable Male

We have spent many pages discussing the choice and conditioning of breeding females prior to and at the time of breeding. Now a few words need to be said about your choice of a sire for the new litter. The indisputable fact is, he will contribute half of the puppies' genetic characteristics.

It goes without saying that you have studied the breed standards and compared them to the conformation, color, and markings of available males. Pedigrees have been studied; if he is a proven sire, his progeny have been evaluated. Final selection might rest on other, rather esoteric values.

• Evaluate his temperament. If possible, meet and handle the prospective sire and all his available adult offspring. Be especially critical of exaggerated aggressiveness or shyness.

• If your bitch has any flaws or faults (heaven forbid!) that have been discovered in the show ring or elsewhere, look for a male that does not duplicate those faults.

This gangly greyhound pup may someday be a race winner or a child's pet.

When evaluating a potential stud dog, identify his faults (there are bound to be a few), and be sure that your bitch does not have similar faults.

• Ask questions about genetic problems known to exist in the breed. That includes joint disease, such as elbow and hip dysplasia in some breeds, ocular deformities or skin-fold problems in others. Some breeds are prone to spinal disc disease; others may have problems with droopy ears. If such conditions are discovered in the prospective sire's background, it is prudent to locate another male.

• Health considerations are extremely important. If breeding to a show animal, you will probably find him in excellent condition. If not, be sure he appears strong and vital. His coat should shine; he should be well muscled and active. His eyes should be clear and bright, and he should display a natural curiosity when you meet him.

Stud Fees and Contracts

Stud fee considerations are in the purview of the dam and sire's owners. Generally, the better a stud has performed in exhibition, the higher his fee. If he has sired class winning offspring or champions, the stud costs may increase also. A proven stud that compliments your bitch's qualities is a bargain, no matter what the fee.

Choice of a sire should never be made on the basis of a low stud fee. Sometimes the fee is negotiable, and if the dam is equal or superior in quality to the sire, a choice of puppies may be made a part of the fee. The fee should always be discussed and committed to writing, signed by both owners, before the bitch is bred.

Always look at the stud's registration paper to assure that he belongs to the person with whom you are negotiating. Check his pedigree and compare it to the other data you have seen and offspring you have handled. Arrive at a definite, written agreement on where the breeding will take place and who will witness it. Note repeat service guarantees in case no pregnancy results. If a kennel boarding fee is to be charged, it should also be stated.

The fee agreement should also address who is responsible for payment for physical examination of the stud. A reproductive physical examination is absolutely essential for a stud if one has not been done within the previous 90 days (see Male Examination, page 48). If you decide an exam is not necessary because of a recent certification of health, read the health report carefully. If it does not specify prostatic and testicular examinations, request a new examination.

If the above recommendations seem like overkill to you, consider your investment in time, money, and love. Don't be intimidated into compromising your standard because of friendship or respect for a person. If the owner of a stud is insulted by your requests and summarily denies them, perhaps you should look for another stud. Handshakes may work for some, but don't depend on it.

Patient Labrador retriever pup, waiting for the games to begin.

Chapter 4
Potential Breeding Problems

Breeding problems include both reversible and permanent conditions—those caused by physical limitations or deformities, as well as actual infertility due to disease (see discussion of Metrites and Brucellosis, page 45) or physiological abnormalities.

Disease

Bitches that cycle erratically or not at all, as well as those that display extended heat periods and other estrus variations, may be infertile. Breeding animals that can't or won't mate, or those that mate without conception may suffer from any number of disease or anatomical problems.

Lack of Human Understanding

Other types of breeding problems are just as real, but are not due to infertility. They are associated with a lack of human understanding of normal canine reproductive features. A bitch that is a problem breeder may be normal in every way except for her refusal to accept a male you have chosen for her. As a

dog breeder, you must understand and learn to deal with that psychological canine phenomenon.

Stress

Another class of reversible breeding problems relates to stress manifested by dogs being mated. When a chosen stud dog is in a distant city, breeders often ship the female to the male by air. Airline travel for kenneled dogs is not terribly risky to their general health, but travel stress-related breeding problems are well recognized by experienced breeders and should be considered when breeding failures occur in commercially shipped dogs. Following an airplane ride, some bitches go out of heat and fail to ovulate. The reason for that phenomenon is thought by many to be a stress-induced hormone change.

Shy Males

Males that are shipped to females for breeding may refuse to mate in strange surroundings. The problem is more prevalent in young, inexperienced stud dogs, and it sometimes even occurs when a male is taken to a female's home or kennel in the family car. It is doubtful if any hormone changes are to blame, but, rather, discomfort and shyness of the male with strange environments and handlers.

Although those examples present problems for dog breeders, they are not necessarily fertility problems. One solution to a shy male is to bring the bitch in heat to him; or instead of shipping a female in season to the male, consider artificial insemination (see page 54), using chilled extended semen. That solution may be no more expensive than her airline ticket, and may yield more gratifying results.

Breeding Records

Complete owner records are essential to any discussion of breeding problems. Bitches' estrus cycles vary from one to another, and if your female's pattern is not accurately documented, little will be gained from the following discussion. Usually, an individual bitch's estrous pattern, once established, will remain constant for her.

Normal estrous cycles occur at fairly regular intervals, have regular, predictable periods of proestrus, estrus, and diestrus, and have anestrus periods of at least 120 days. Normal cycles, except in basenjis, repeat in less than one year.

Make permanent records of the date your bitch first displays signs of proestrus, the color and quantity of vaginal discharge, duration of the discharge, attitude changes,appetite aberrations, and any other physical or attitude signals you might note.

Silent Heats

One of the most perplexing problems a dog breeder faces is a bitch that shows no outward signs of estrus (silent heat). She may be several years old without ever showing the typical genital swelling or bloody discharge. Some animal health professionals believe that silent heats do not occur, but, rather, unobservant owners miss the signs. When owners live with an intact bitch in their home, it is unlikely that they will miss spots of bloody discharge on a tile floor. The attitude changes typical of a bitch in season are also difficult to overlook!

When anxiously waiting for their bitch to show signs of proestrus, I

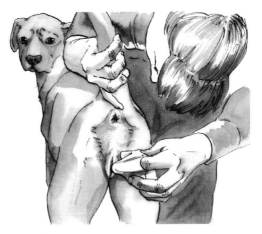

Blot vulva with tissue to find traces of first proestrus bleeding.

advise prospective dog breeders to blot a white facial tissue against the bitch's vulva every few days. When no signs of bloody discharge are seen for a year, silent heat must be assumed.

My experience leads me to believe that unapparent estrus is rare, but it does occur. It seems to happen more commonly in bitches that are housed in apartments, totally removed from all other dogs.

If silent heats are suspected, an expert in canine theriogenology (the study of reproduction) should be consulted. Often, extensive serum hormone level testing is necessary to determine the cause of the problem. Sometimes, progesterone hormone levels are assayed each month. Periodic blood tests may be combined with microscopic examination of vaginal smears taken every ten days. Ultrasound images of her reproductive organs are studied and laparoscopic examination of the ovaries may be considered.

Cause

The cause of unapparent estrus is infrequently determined. Sometimes a bitch that appears to have no estrus cycle is actually in anestrus. That situation can be ruled out by careful observation for six months.

Of vital importance is thoughtful evaluation of her complete medical history, especially if she was acquired as an adult. Androgens (male hormones) or other anabolic steroids that were administered in the past can result in anestrus. Glu-cocorticoids are another type of hormone that are sometimes used to treat dermatitis or other diseases and may result in anestrus.

Sometimes, bitches are given progesterone to prevent estrus for a short period of time, but instead, its effect is extremely long lasting. It may be many months or even a year or two before normal estrous cycles resume.

Certain ovarian tumors and cysts may cause an overproduction of progesterone, leaving a female in a continual state of diestrus that appears to be anestrus. Such ovarian conditions may be diagnosed by ultrasound imaging, by serum progesterone determinations, or by exploratory surgery or laparoscopy.

Hermaphrodites are animals that may appear to be normal females, though they possess both male and female sexual organs. They often have no gross male reproductive characteristics, but they fail to exhibit an estrous cycle. A thorough clinical physical examination may diagnose hermaphroditism in some cases. In others, chromosome studies are required.

Solutions

In some cases of silent heat, the problem may be solved without diagnosis of the cause. There are two techniques that might be tried:
• The first technique is to borrow a compatible intact bitch that cycles regularly, and normally exhibits all phases of the estrous

cycle. House the two dogs together and watch for results. When the newly introduced female shows signs of proestrus, begin close observation of the problem dog. In many cases, the cycling bitch will induce a normal proestrus in the previously silent one.

• Another technique is to house the silent female with a proven fertile breeding male, 24 hours a day for perhaps six months. One day she announces their successful mating by displaying an abdomen enlarged with puppies. Predicting whelping time is sometimes tricky if she is more than four weeks into her gestation before pregnancy is recognized. The good news is that she is bred and will probably exhibit normal estrus signs with her first post-whelping estrous cycle.

In both the above remedies there is a second factor that may influence the results. You have removed a common cause for silent heats. Your bitch is no longer isolated and now has a second dog in her environment.

Spayed bitches show no signs of estrus, and when searching for causes of silent heat, that possibility must be explored as well, especially when the dog was acquired as an adult.

Conformation Influences

By virtue of their conformation, a few breeds are predisposed to breeding problems. The muscle mass in some tiny breeds is so undeveloped, and skeletal construction is so delicate, that males lack the physical strength, athletic ability, and endurance necessary to mount and breed a female. Likewise, some females are so frail they can't support the weight of a male. The teacup-sized toy breeds are especially subject to those kinds of conformational breeding problems.

Considering their elongated bodies and short legs, it is little wonder that dachshund, basset hound, and Welsh corgi males occasionally require assistance when attempting to breed a female, especially if she is taller than he is.

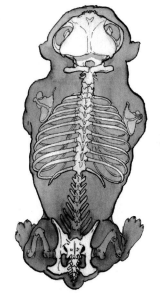

Size disparity between dam's narrow pelvis and puppies' thick head and shoulders makes natural bulldog whelping nearly impossible.

Females of very heavy-chested breeds, such as English bulldogs, sometimes have difficulty supporting the weight of a male, and human help is often required to successfully accomplish the breeding act. Similar problems are reported in heavy-bodied, short-legged basset hounds. When a male mounts, the female sits down due to the weight on her hind legs. To further complicate basset hound breeding, many females have an apron of fat and loose skin that drapes downward over their vulvas, effectively preventing normal, unassisted intromission (male penis introduction into the vaginal tract).

Given the situations just mentioned, and others, it seems we have created breeds that might die out in the absence of human intervention. Hand-breeding and artificial insemination are sometimes the only ways to propagate animals that are unable to mate naturally due to lack of condition and physi-

Assisting breeding by supporting female.

cal, conformational problems (see Artificial Insemination, page 54).

Example: I chuckle when I think about the occasional difficulty encountered when attempting to breed animals with exaggerated phenotypes (physical appearance). A close friend and client once presented a six-week-old litter of puppies for examination and vaccinations. Their mother was a valuable golden retriever. The pups sported long wavy coats of a golden red color, but they all had exceedingly elongated bodies and short legs. They looked like they were walking in a trench. They were strong, healthy, and full of mischief as they scurried around the exam room floor on their stubby little legs, looking like wriggly little overgrown caterpillars.

My friend confirmed that his next door neighbor owned a longhaired miniature dachshund male. He said that Schnitzel retained his ancestral badger hunting and tunneling expertise. He held the six-foot (1.83 m) wooden backyard fence in total disdain. The little dachshund was discovered in the retriever's yard several times while she was in heat. Logically, no significance was placed on his presence since he was obviously too short in stature to mount the mature retriever bitch. That was a gross misassumption that was not repeated the next time she came into heat!

It should be noted that the problems we have been discussing are associated with both hereditary conformation of the animals and their physical condition. Trim and muscled, well-exercised, athletic dogs of any breed are less likely to present breeding problems than those that have grown soft and obese from too many treats and too few Frisbee games in the yard or long walks in the park.

Female Breeding Failures

The single most frequent cause of breeding failures is improper timing. Canine ovulation is spontaneous, and only occurs once during an estrous cycle; therefore, timing should receive maximum consideration in your breeding program.

When a female shows all the typical signs of proestrus and estrus, she will stand for a male when the right time arrives, right? Usually, but not always.

Refusal

Mate refusal may (in rare instances) be related to a lack of socialization of the dog. Either a male or female that is raised apart from all other canines may not recognize a potential mate as a member of its species. Thus, when introduced to a prospective mate, complete rejection results. That previously remote possibility may be increasing in totally isolated, urban apartment pets.

Behavioral peculiarities can cause females to refuse certain males.

Natural breeding may be impossible when mates are of disproportional sizes.

Bitches may have nothing to do with males that have been carefully qualified and selected as mates. That attitude is poorly understood by breeders and reproductive specialists alike. Some speculate that the females consider themselves to be the dominant members of their packs, and they refuse to submit their bodies to subordinate animals.

Sometimes those bitches are muzzled and held while their undesirable suitors complete their parts of the mating acts. Since those females haven't exhibited typical standing heat, forced breeding of that nature may easily be ill timed. Timing is critical and should probably be determined through vaginal smears and serum progesterone hormone levels.

In any breed, but especially in toys, females' dispositions may deter from natural breeding. They will not allow any male to mount them, regardless of all normal outward signs of estrus. Biologically, those females are ready, but mentally they will not receive males. That idiosyncrasy is frequently seen in bitches that are raised from puppyhood with their prospective mates.

Sometimes, refusal breeding problems can be solved by using a different male. In other cases, artificial insemination might be the answer. Appropriate timing for forced breeding or artificial insemination is critical. I have often pondered the wisdom of overriding the refusal attitude of a female. Perhaps she somehow possesses information we lack?

Size Difference

Dogs at the opposite ends of the size and weight scale may not recognize each other as potential mates. I sincerely doubt that any

self-respecting Great Dane or Newfoundland is apt to become aroused
by a Chihuahua in heat!

Physical Abnormalities

If a female exhibits normal physical signs of proestrus—flirts, flags her
tail and teases a male during estrus,
and allows him to mount but cries or
jumps aside when he begins to penetrate, the problem might be physical.
The possibilities are numerous. She
may have a vaginal obstruction (see
Persistent Hymen, page 47) such as
a partial vaginal prolapse, or an infantile or underdeveloped genital tract.
Most small-animal veterinarians are
capable of diagnosing and treating
these physical problems.

Examination for congenital
abnormalities of the female reproductive tract is best done during
estrus. A stricture may require a
general anesthetic to correct surgically or by dilation. Sometimes,
instead of correcting the problem,
artificial insemination is done. In
those cases, it is best to tentatively
schedule a cesarean section at the
same time.

Another reason for females'
refusal to breed during an apparently normal heat may be associated with a false or split heat. The
remedy is to wait until the normal
heat begins, and try again.

Acceptance without Conception

Parts of this subject are also covered in the next chapter that deals

Same species, anatomically quite different.

with pre-breeding physical examinations and breeding processes.

Vaginal Cytology

If a potential brood bitch experiences outwardly normal estrus
cycles but does not conceive when
bred, consult your veterinarian, who
will no doubt recommend vaginal
cytology. (Cytology refers to the
study of tissue cells.) The technique
entails the use of a series of smears,
painlessly obtained using cotton
swabs, over a period of several
days from the bitch's vagina. The
daily swab samples are smeared on
glass microscope slides and
stained. Cell types are then identified and studied under a high mag-
nification laboratory microscope.

Changing cell types are used to
predict approximately when ovulation takes place, thereby improving

Five-week-old doberman pinscher puppies, really getting into the feeding program.

the possibility of successful breeding or artificial insemination. An individual's ovulation and receptive period may be very early or very late during the estrus period. Vaginal cytology should help to establish appropriate breeding time.

Need for Hormone Analysis

Other techniques such as hormone studies are sometimes employed to establish a bitch's ovulation date. Blood samples are taken and levels of estrogen, progesterone, and LH are determined. Those studies are only feasible if suitable laboratory facilities are readily available.

If her hormone levels cycle normally and her vaginal smear analy-sis correlates, it is possible that ovulation fails to occur. In such cases, laparoscopy may be the diagnostic tool of choice. Blood testing and laparoscopic techniques are expensive and are usually reserved for very valuable breeding animals. When needed, services of those types are available from veterinary theriogenologists who can be found in urban specialty practices or veterinary colleges.

Ovarian Fragments

An infrequent cause of normal appearing estrus cycles without conception is a post-spay ovarian fragment.

Example: A client obtained a bitch from a city newspaper advertisement. She was purchased as a breeding and hunting dog, and appeared to be a purebred Labrador retriever. The new owner purposefully bred her to another young hunting dog. No puppies resulted from the breeding, but, undaunted, on her next cycle the owner bred her again, this time to a proven Labrador stud. She again failed to conceive, and when in proestrus six months later, she was presented for fertility examination. A small area of her abdomen was shaved and cleaned, and a two-inch (50.8 cm) scar was identified on the midline, just behind her navel. It certainly appeared to be a typical spay incision scar.

The client was advised that we were probably dealing with a piece of ovary that was left in her abdomen at the time she was spayed. The ovarian fragment was apparently large enough to simulate all the typical signs of a normal estrous cycle.

Our options were abdominal X-rays, laboratory serum hormone levels determination, vaginal cytology, or exploratory surgery. Without further examination or discussion, the owner requested an exploratory laparotomy to confirm the diagnosis and to try to locate and remove the ovarian tissue, if that was the problem.

A fragment of ovarian tissue about the size of a large pea was located immediately behind the dog's right kidney. A good-sized portion of the uterine body and a small piece of one uterine horn was also found. There was no way to regain breeding status in the bitch, but we did stop her ineffective estrus cycle by finishing the ovariohysterectomy someone else started.

Injuries

Previous physical injuries such as pelvic fractures, hip injuries, and hind leg ligament damage may interfere with a bitch's ability to support the weight of a male. If injuries of those types are not well healed, postpone breeding her until her next estrus cycle. If joint problems are congenital in nature and not the result of injury, you should study their hereditability and reconsider the use of the bitch in your breeding program altogether.

Stifle (knee) injuries such as collateral ligament ruptures, patellar (kneecap) dislocations, and perhaps even anterior cruciate ligament ruptures may be associated with skeleton conformation faults. Before a male or female with stifle injuries or problems is included in your breeding program, check the genetics of the condition.

A word of caution: Often, when artificial insemination is used, it effectively overrides some natural obstacle to propagation of that animal's genotype (genetic makeup). In other words, when you artificially inseminate, you may be artificially perpetuating abnormalities that would otherwise prevent a bitch from being bred. If that activity is continued, you may promote or create a bloodline of invalids.

Persistent Estrus

Persistent estrus is another problem that is occasionally encountered in brood bitches. Affected females show permanent signs of estrus, complete with vaginal discharge, genital swelling, and even male receptivity. If an estrus period persists for over four weeks, your veterinarian should be consulted. The cause of persistent estrus may be an ovarian follicular cyst or certain ovarian tumors. Specialized diagnostic testing with hormonal assays, ultrasound imaging, and sometimes laparoscopy may help devise a successful treatment scheme.

Hormonal Problems

Although menopause is not seen in canines, older dogs experience infrequent estrous cycles and conception failures. They are also more prone to various reproductive disorders (see Chapter 14, beginning on page 159).

Other breeding failures and infertility problems include those associated with *hypothyroidism*, which is accompanied by many other signs and symptoms.

Hypoluteodism is an endocrine-related condition that is often suspected but rarely diagnosed. It may occur secondary to cystic ovaries and can sometimes be presumptively diagnosed by hormone analysis and ultrasound imaging. It is mentioned here only because it often finds its way into dog breeding literature.

A discussion of infertility and breeding problems of females would not be complete without mentioning a condition I worked with on several occasions in our general practice. Every few years I was asked to help establish a normal estrous cycle in a bitch so she could be bred. The animals were assumed by their owners to be undergoing silent heats. Upon exam, the dogs appeared quite normal. At three to six years of age, they exhibited no signs of mammary development that is characteristic of cycling females. External genitalia was immature, even infantile in some cases. They were usually housed with other dogs, but showed no signs of heat over a year or more.

In those days, serum hormone assays were not standardized nor in use except in the universities. Ultrasound imaging was still in the future. In each case, after considerable study and inquiry (and once exploratory surgery), the bitches were discovered to be normal spayed females.

Male Refusal or Inability to Breed

A male that is raised and housed with a female may elect not to breed her when she is in season and receptive. She may flirt and attempt to seduce him with all her canine feminine wiles, to no avail. Such reluctance is often associated with earlier encounters when he attempted to mount her when she was not in heat, and was firmly rejected and sent to the showers. Having received a few severe rejections, he doesn't trust his instincts when the appropriate time arrives for amorous advances and is therefore unable to perform.

Physical Problems

When a male mounts a bitch in season, then suddenly dismounts, an examination of his reproductive organs should be performed. Sometimes a minor deformity of the penis causes pain when intromission is attempted. A tissue remnant (see explanation of persistent frenulum, page 49) leading backward from the glans penis to the penile shaft causes the glans to be pulled down and back as he attempts intromission. The problem can usually be quickly solved by your veterinarian with a local anesthetic, a snip with scissors, and cautery.

Obstruction

Another common problem in long-haired breeds is the presence of foreign material inside the bitch's genital tract. Long hairs may fold into the vulva, irritate, and sometimes even lacerate the male's delicate, sensitive glans penis tissue. That problem will be averted when a thorough pre-breeding examination is done on the bitch.

Self-tie

In natural breeding, a dog's penis finds its way into the female's vulva

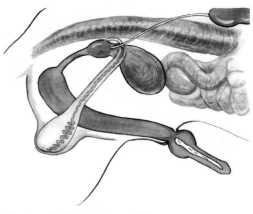
Erect penis, illustrating self-tie.

somewhat by trial and error. An inexperienced, excited male, full of vim and vinegar, often tries too hard. After he has mounted and energetically but unsuccessfully gone through the motions a few times, he may self-tie (see Chapter 5, Breeding Process, beginning on page 50), ejaculate, and temporarily lose interest in the female. That effectively finishes him for an hour or two while nature restores his organs to their useful status again.

Conception Failure

When conception does not occur with a normal, natural breeding, a physical examination and semen evaluation should be performed on the male if it was not done prior to breeding. An unproven male of any age may be sterile. His age or condition may render his production of viable sperm too low to effectively impregnate a bitch. There are several diseases capable of causing

43

Veterinary physical exams of both breeding animals is sound management.

problems, and specific diagnosis is important.

Prostatic Disease

Many males over six years of age have clinical prostate gland enlargement (see Brucellosis, page 45). Prostatitis, or prostate gland infection, may account for bacteria being shed into the animal's semen. Bacterial presence may account for intermittent sterility in a male. With any conception failure, it is prudent to collect and evaluate the stud's semen, checking for viability and motility of sperms cells. If the sample is collected under aseptic conditions, a bacterial culture may be done as well.

If a thorough pre-breeding examination was performed, prostatic disease should have been identified at that time, and that male should not have been used.

Rarely is a canine stud overused to the point that his semen concentration and sperm vitality is reduced below acceptable levels, but that is another possible cause for breeding failure.

Pre-breeding Evaluation

Before breeding, both male and female should be physically examined, preferably by the same professional. Before the exam, the veterinarian should be furnished with breeding and health histories of both animals. The clinician should review references discussing genetic problems to which your particular breed is predisposed. The examiner should be especially mindful of minor physical or physiological problems that might have little or no consequence in a pet, but could be passed to the progeny of the planned mating.

Breed Faults

It is also an excellent idea to have both breeding animals "faulted" by an experienced breeder or judge of the breed. Such an evaluation of minor "show faults" of the breed may prevent the propagation or escalation of those flaws. For example, slightly reduced pigmentation of the muzzle, eyelids, or iris might be considered a minor show fault. If a bitch with that fault is bred to a male with a similar fault, it may surface in the puppies as a serious photosensitivity problem that is difficult to eliminate from the bloodline.

Tail carriage, length of neck, ear set, and a hundred other features are described in the breed standard. Slight deviations from the perfect is expected, but if both sire and dam carry the same minor imperfections, the progeny may exhibit major faults.

Congenital Diseases

In many breeds of dogs, the veterinarian will want to examine for, or see certifications of, normal hip conformation. The list of breeds afflicted with hip dysplasia seems to grow annually. It is especially prevalent in German shepherds, hunting breeds, and most giant and working breeds, but is also seen in many others, including toys and terriers.

In some animals, such as collies, Australian shepherds, shelties, poodles, cockers, and several hunting breeds, certification of normal eyes (retinal diseases) may be an important consideration.

Breeding malamutes should be certified free of dwarfism (achondrodysplasia). West Highland white, Scottish, and cairn terriers might be certified free of jawbone disease (craniomandibular osteopathy). Newfoundlands are sometimes examined for, or certified free of, a vascular disorder known as subaortic stenosis.

In some breeds, minor dental deformities might be overlooked in a single pet, but they can be exaggerated in the puppies if present in both parents.

Brace of mischievous King Charles spaniel pups.

Infectious Diseases

All infectious diseases are important, and your veterinarian's examination will establish the breeding animals' good health and freedom from illness. The following specific reproductive diseases also demand particular attention.

Brucellosis. This chronic canine bacterial infection causes infertility and abortion. It is often insidious, with no outward signs in the female, but is usually accompanied by physical signs in the infected male.

Clinical signs in a male may include apparent swelling of either or both testicles (primarily, swelling of the epididymis, the tube leading from the testicle to the vas deferens). A short time later, either one or both testicles begin to atrophy

A proud pug dam and her litter of fat little puglets.

(decrease in size and become soft). Sometimes, painful orchitis (testicular inflammation) is evident.

An infected dog's sperm cells are usually grossly abnormal in both physical appearance and mobility when examined under a microscope, and his semen will contain numerous white blood cells. On physical examination, veterinarians will usually also discover regional lymph node enlargement.

Unfortunately, an infected male is sometimes only identified and diagnosed after he has been bred to several bitches that abort or fail to conceive. By that time, the bred females are also lifetime carriers of the infection.

A blood test will detect an infected animal, and could prevent an infection from spreading from either of the prospective breeding animals to the other. Once contracted, Brucellosis virtually ends the reproductive career of both males and females.

Vaginitis. Vaginal inflammation or infections are not major problems in canines, and when they occur, they rarely cause systemic illness. Vaginitis is most common in a very mild form in young females before their first estrous cycle. Cultures may be made to isolate bacterial causes for the condition, but culturing the bitch's vagina is problematical due to the variety of normal bacterial residents. Treatment of prepuberal vaginitis is rarely necessary or effective. The signs usually subside and disappear before proestrus begins.

The significance of vaginitis in breeding animals is related to the possibility of causative bacteria migrating into the uterus when the cervix is dilated during estrus. The infection may also alter the normal pH (acidity) of the females' genital vaults, thereby killing sperm cells or reducing their vitality.

Many times, when treatment is deemed necessary, an antiseptic douche is effective, using such products as dilute povidone iodine solution, or a nitrofuran. Those or other similar drugs can also kill sperm, and they must be carefully evaluated before being used in a breeding bitch. Diagnosis and treatment of vaginitis should be left to veterinary clinicians.

Herpes. A herpes virus can cause blister-like lesions on the mucous membrane surfaces of male and female genitalia. Canine herpes virus is host-specific for the dog, and it can cause abortion or lack of conception. It is spread from animal to animal through the breeding process, and can also infect puppies at birth. It is a true venereal disease of dogs. I know of no reliably successful treatment, although new drugs have been released that may be effective. Your veterinarian is best equipped to advise you on an appropriate course of action.

Hyperplasia

Vaginal hyperplasia is a noninfectious condition that interferes with mating. Artificial insemination is usually required if the bitch is to be bred while the condition exists. It appears as a thick, tongue-like fold of the floor of the vagina that protrudes outward through the lips of the vulva. It is sometimes mistaken for vaginal prolapse. It usually occurs in a young bitch during her first or second proestrus. Treatment is sometimes possible using topical ointments, but severe cases require surgical intervention.

History and Examination

Health and breeding histories will reveal the use of drugs that may affect a male's sperm or a bitch's ovulation. Advanced age or a history of prior breeding failures of a male might suggest the need for semen evaluation prior to breeding.

A previous breeding failure of a female may stimulate the use of vaginal cytology or hormone analysis to improve breeding timing and

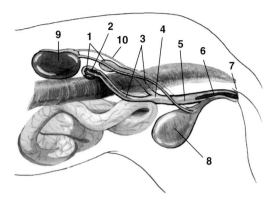

increase the likelihood of conception. Advanced age in a bitch (over six or seven years in average-sized dogs) usually suggests a blood count and biochemical profile prior to breeding.

Female Examination

A bitch's genital tract can be examined without pain or sedation. Visual examination of the vulva, vestibule, and vagina is usually accomplished using a lighted scope of various designs. Digital examination of a virgin bitch's external genitalia with a gloved, lubricated finger might reveal a persistent hymen, vaginal stricture, or bands of vaginal tissue that can cause obstruction or reluctance to breed.

Those features are non-health-threatening, and are usually corrected by minor surgery. If left uncorrected, the female may wince, cry, or sit down upon attempted intromission by the male. The male may experience pain to his penis from the vaginal strictures or

Female reproductive and urinary anatomy:
1. *Ovaries*
2. *Oviduct or fallopian tube*
3. *Uterine horns*
4. *Uterine body*
5. *Cervix*
6. *Vagina*
7. *Vulva*
8. *Urinary bladder*
9. *Kidney*
10. *Ureter*

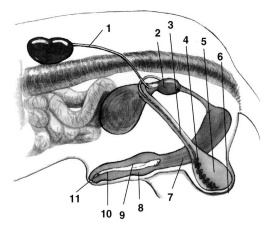

bands, and thereafter refuse to breed her.

In valuable bitches with a history of prior breeding failures, the veterinarian might suggest abdominal X-rays or ultrasound examination of the uterus and ovaries. In some cases, fiber optic instruments are employed to actually visualize the reproductive organs by means of laparoscopy. Those techniques can be very rewarding in the hands of a canine reproduction specialist.

Male Examination

A male's reproductive organs are more easily examined than a female's. Abnormalities of testicles and epididymus (the tube carrying sperm from the testicle to the vas deferens) are easily perceived by visual exam and palpation with practiced fingers.

Retained testicles. In rare instances, a monorchid male (one that has only one testicle in the scrotum) will be offered as a stud.

Monorchidism and cryptorchidism (neither testicle in the scrotum) are congenital, hereditary problems occasionally seen in all breeds. Either condition is very undesirable in any dog. Retained testicles eliminate animals from all conformation show rings, although affected animals can compete in some performance trials under certain conditions.

Male dogs are born with their testicles positioned in their abdomens. By the time puppies are 30 days old, both testicles should be descended into their scrotums. Failure to descend seems to have very complex causes. The problem is hereditary, but the genetic mechanism is poorly understood.

Both monorchidism and cryptorchidism occur more commonly in purebred dogs than in mixed breeds. Seventy-five percent of all dogs with retained testicles are monorchids. In monorchids, twice as many right testicles are retained in the abdomen than left ones.

Males with both testicles retained in the abdomen are typically sterile but not impotent. Most monorchids are both virile and fertile.

Testicular retention constitutes a major fault in all purebred dogs, and no clear-thinking dog breeder will consider using a monorchid stud. Any dog (purebred or mixed) with one or both testicles undescended should be castrated at puberty or before he is two years old. Retained testicles often develop tumors, many of which are malignant.

Prostatic disease. A digital rectal examination will reveal prostate enlargement or irregularities. That part of an examination is of greatest importance in males past middle age, but it should be done routinely in all breeding males. Discovery of prostatic infection in a prospective stud should instantly eliminate that dog from use.

In some cases, treatment may be possible (unless the cause is Brucellosis). When treatment is initiated, the antibiotics used may affect the viability of sperm cells. A stud with prostatic disease should not be considered for future breeding use unless the condition is resolved and a subsequent normal semen analysis is performed.

Penis examination. The male's penis is easily examined for persistent frenulum, which is a tissue band leading backward and downward from the bottom of the tip of the glans penis. If it exists, the frenulum can be surgically eliminated using local anesthesia. Without correction, intromission may be impossible or so painful as to interfere with normal breeding.

- **Os penis.** The rather unique canine penis contains a bone called the *os penis*; it extends from very near the tip of the glans penis backward through the soft tissue of the penile shaft. The purpose of the os penis is to aim the male's non-erect penis, directing it into the bitch's vulva and vagina. (The process is discussed on page 51.) Sometimes male breeding failures are associated with an os penis that does not reach far enough forward into the soft glans penis tissue. In those cases, the glans penis folds back and intromission is rarely achieved.

- **Bulbus glandis.** Another unique canine male reproductive structure is the bulbus glandis. Located toward the rear of the shaft of the penis, it is an important part of penis erection and the entire breeding process. The bulbus glandis begins to engorge with blood as soon as intromission is accomplished. The bulb swells quickly and forms a firm, almost spherical enlargement easily twice the diameter of the remainder of the penis shaft.

Histories

Both veterinarians and breeder consultants will be interested in reproductive histories of the animals. If it is the first breeding of a male or female, their physical maturity is important. If either or both have previously been bred, the dates, number, and health of puppies produced will be of particular interest.

Chapter 5
Breeding Process

Canines possess strong natural reproductive instincts and capabilities. A normal, healthy male and a normal female in season will usually have no difficulty mating if relatively equal in size.

Since we are managing or stewarding our canine population, it is our intention to breed the right dog to the right bitch. Our hope and intention is to produce healthy puppies that are a credit to the breed. If possible, we wish to improve the breed.

Breed standards have been studied, your mature bitch is nearing proestrus and a male has been tentatively selected to sire the litter; it is time to plan the actual mating.

Introducing the Mates

Avoid a circus atmosphere. While it is a good idea to witness the breeding act, the fewer humans present at mating time, the better. If one or both animals have previously mated, the process will probably proceed smoothly. If both are inexperienced, help may be necessary. Usually, however, no encouragement or participation is required or advised.

Typically, a bitch in estrus near ovulation time flags her tail, elevates her rear in the face of the male (see Estrus, "Standing Heat," pages 8–9), then bounces around, flirting unashamedly. She may lick the male's genital area, sniff, and even try to mount him.

A mature macho male usually walks around on stiff legs, ears erect, flattered by the female's attention. He will lick her vulva and eventually mount her hindquarters, placing one of his forelegs on each side of her back. Experienced stud dogs usually move very carefully at

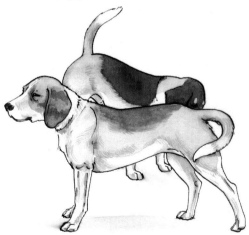

Female shows readiness to breed by flagging tail held to side.

first, mounting the female from the rear. Younger males often begin by mounting the female's neck, and fumble their way back to the appropriate position.

Mounting and dismounting may be repeated several times before actual breeding takes place. She may shy away when he mounts, then begin to flirt again. This canine foreplay sometimes lasts a minute or two, sometimes an hour. If neither is snapping at the other or showing severe rejection signs, don't interfere.

The Breeding Act

When convinced they are suited for each other, the bitch stands quietly and allows the male to mount her. After he places his forelegs on either side of her rib cage, he steps forward with his hind legs, which positions his prepuce in close proximity behind her vulva. She elevates her hindquarters, tipping her front quarters downward.

The male's penis is not yet erect, but the os penis directs the glans penis into her vulva and promotes entry of the shaft of the penis. As the supersensitive glans penis enters the vulva, the male will slide his forelegs backward into the flanks of the bitch, gripping her tightly just in front of her hind legs.

Standing nearly erect behind her, he then thrusts with his hindquarters to accomplish intromission, pressing the penis into her vagina.

Posture of breeding pair during intromission.

The female may experience some discomfort at that time, but it is minor if she is mature and her reproductive tract is normal.

The Tie

Once intromission is accomplished, as the penis extends fully into her vagina, its vascular structure engorges, and it becomes erect. The bulbus glandis swells well inside the vagina, in front of the contracting bands of vaginal tissue (constrictor vestibuli muscles), and the two are tied together.

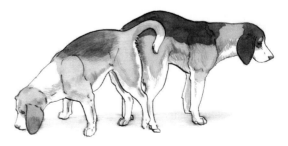

Typical posture of breeding pair during tie.

The male may continue thrusting motions for a few seconds, then relax for a minute or two. Next, he brings one foreleg over the bitch's back and briefly stands beside her, with their genital organs still joined. One of the two soon swings its body so they are facing in opposite directions, tied together with their rumps touching. The male's penis, now directed posteriorly, is still held within the female's vagina by the engorged bulbus glandis.

Because ejaculation continues the entire time the dogs are tied, the duration of a tie is often cited by dog breeders as having some great significance in the number of puppies produced from a mating. I have known many large healthy litters resulting from a single mating wherein the tie only lasted a minute or two. Other small litters have resulted from matings that were repeated 3 or 4 times, with ties of 20 minutes each.

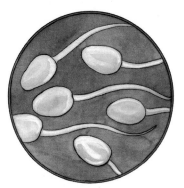

Sperm cells or male gametes are observed microscopically for motility and conformation.

Semen Composition

The first portion of semen is produced by the male's prostate gland. It is only about .5 cc in volume (in an average-sized hunting dog) and quite thin in consistency. It takes about half a minute to produce.

The second fraction of ejaculate, immediately following the first, is thick and white. It contains the most active and concentrated numbers of sperm. Its volume is about 1 cc and it takes only a minute or two to complete.

The third fraction of semen also originates from the prostate gland and constitutes the major portion of the ejaculate. Sometimes containing more than an ounce of fluid, it is produced over a span of 5 to 45 minutes.

As you can see, it is unlikely that the duration of a tie beyond that first few minutes is terribly important, but it makes for excellent conversation among dog breeders.

Duration of the Tie

The tie normally lasts from a minute or two to perhaps 30 or 40 minutes. If tied for more than an hour, contact your veterinarian. On rare occasions, the male or female may fall down or lie down while tied. In the process of getting up, they may cause a full twist or torsion in the shaft of the penis. In such an extremely unlikely event, the bulbus glandis may remain engorged, the duration of the tie is greatly extended, and severe damage to either the male or female may result.

Do not interfere with a tie. Inexperienced owners often try to relieve the perceived distress of either the male or female, and begin coaxing the animals, causing them to try to walk about. Since dogs are not notably adept at backing up, pulling one another about causes both of them more discomfort than if left quiet. Canine breeding ties are absolutely normal and are an integral part of canine species propagation. Do not throw water on them, try to pull them apart, or otherwise interfere unless the time of the tie is extended well above normal. Before acting in any way, seek the advice of your veterinarian.

Assisted Breeding

Assistance may be rendered to a mating pair to help educate inexperienced young breeding animals. Holding the collar and reassuring a finicky or frightened, squirmy bitch (see diagram, page 36) is sometimes necessary to expedite the breeding process and assure that a natural breeding is accomplished. An overanxious, energetic male sometimes appreciates help in directing his penis into the bitch's vagina. Using your hand to support the posterior abdomen (see diagram, page 36) of a lightweight bitch being bred by a larger male will give comfort and assurance to both. Each of those little aids to breeding is easily accomplished and neither reflect human interference in natural selection or reproduction of the animals.

In some breeds previously mentioned, hand-breeding or artificial breeding is necessary for propagation of the bloodline. Following assisted breeding, the puppies conceived are often delivered by cesarean section. Left on their own, those dogs might never reproduce. Due to their size, strength, or conformation, their little branch of the canine tree would wilt and die in one generation without human intervention.

In those situations, you are not simply assisting, you are enabling their reproduction. When you thus intrude in the canine breeding act, you must accept the fact that you are responsible for the production of puppies that would not be conceived naturally. Give careful thought and consideration to that fact. To artificially or hand-breed animals that are congenitally unable to reproduce without human intervention is not likely to have a long-term positive effect on any breed.

Post-breeding Examination

Since the unique and fascinating mating act just described is normal and natural, one expects to find no injury to either dog. After mating, females should be checked over visually for signs of damage to their reproductive organs. Rarely, small wounds are found in the vulva. Except for swelling and redness of

This Jack Russell terrier dam's abdomen is distended with puppies, and her glands are full of milk.

their external genitalia, no abnormalities should be present.

Likewise, a male's penis will appear inflamed and swollen for a few hours following tie-breeding, but injury is uncommon. Once in a while, a female may turn and snap at a male when he begins to mount her. In such cases, you should check him for puncture wounds, especially in his prepuce (sheath).

Artificial Insemination (A.I.)

There are many excellent reasons to use A.I. in a purebred dog breeding program. They include:

- use of an excellent quality male who has suffered a hip, hind leg, spinal, or pelvic injury that prevents him from breeding a bitch naturally;
- use of a top male that lives in another part of the world. His semen may be collected and preserved by a knowledgeable theriogenologist (reproductive

specialist) and shipped to a qualified technician in your area who then inseminates your bitch;

- breeding to an aged or deceased male whose semen was frozen and stored for future use;
- locating and using frozen semen from top-quality males of rare breeds. This concept reflects the ability to avoid inbreeding of animals with very small available gene pools.

A technical discussion of artificial insemination is not in the scope of this book; however, be advised that collection of semen from most males is easily accomplished. Extending and preserving the semen for future use and shipment is a well-established science in itself.

If you plan to collect semen from a male and immediately inseminate your bitch by yourself, be sure you have been thoroughly instructed by a veterinarian or a qualified A.I. technician. Both collection and insemination techniques must be carried out under medically clean circumstances. Proper washing of the animals and sterilization of the collection and insemination equipment is critical.

A.I. is a wonderful tool, but like others, if misused, the results can be disastrous. Uterine infections and injuries to the vulva, vagina, cervix, or uterus often result from inexperienced owners or poor insemination techniques.

I once surgically removed several glass shards from the vagina, cervix, and vulva of a bitch after a glass pipette was employed as the delivery

Two days later, she relaxes as her hungry brood nurses.

tube in an unwise effort to inseminate a frightened, wriggly female that could not be bred to an excited young male. The untrained but persistent owners paid a very high price for their futile attempts to hurry a breeding.

For information about a home-managed artificial insemination program, I suggest you first consult your veterinarian. If further informa-tion is desired, you might contact the nearest college of veterinary medicine and speak to the resident canine reproductive specialist. Another contact for names of nearby specialists is the American College of Theriogenologists and Society for Theriogenology (2727 W. 2nd, P.O. Box 2118, Hastings, Nebraska 69902-2118).

Chapter 6

Pregnancy

The terms *gestation* and *pregnancy* are almost interchangeable. Both refer to the physical and physiological state of females carrying their young. The terms *whelp*, *delivery*, and *parturition* all refer to the production of puppies at the termination of pregnancy.

Duration of Pregnancy

The period of gestation extends from the time of successful mating to parturition. That time has been reported to vary from 56 to 68 or 72 days, depending on the reference. In my experience, average canine gestation is 63 days. The extremes of the wide range quoted are rarely seen, but I know bitches that routinely exhibit a 68-day gestation from breeding date to whelping date.

Technically, the time from the LH hormone peak in a bitch's blood until parturition is consistently between 64 and 66 days. Ovulation occurs two days after the LH peak; therefore, from ovulation to whelping is likely to be 63 days, even though bitches may be mated several days before and after their ovulation dates.

Ova may not be sufficiently mature to unite with sperm cells for two or three days. Ovulation and fertilization times, as related to a bitch's serum hormone levels, are extremely constant in the canine species in general. It is believed that gestation is equally constant in practically all dogs, when based on purely technical evidence.

Variations

One reason for the great range of reported gestation times is that behavioral estrus, or the duration of a particular female's receptivity, may be lengthy. Bitches may stand and receive a male for as long as four or five days before and after the LH hormone peaks in their bloodstreams. Due to the viability time of sperm and ova, fertilization may occur early or late in a "standing heat."

From an owner's point of view, one bitch may always deliver her puppies 59 days from the date of breeding, and another has a perceived gestation of 65 days. In reality, the variation probably has more to do with their individual behavioral estrus periods than actual gestation.

In the real world of dog breeding, few of us enlist the aid of a reproductive specialist to determine a bitch's LH peak, as laboratory analysis is expensive, and if an animal is not a problem breeder, little purpose is served by such exercises.

Whelping Date Estimation

Excellent information about ovulation times has been obtained, documented, and employed by veterinarians and breeders, using vaginal smears instead of hormone analysis. While vaginal cytology (microscopic study of cells) is not as exact as hormone analysis, it is a simple, inexpensive procedure that is used to closely estimate ovulation dates and best days for breeding. Likewise, it is used to predict the approximate date of whelping.

Most small-animal clinicians are well versed in techniques of obtaining and interpreting vaginal smears. Many veterinarians instruct their clients to use swabs and make microscope-slide smears at home. The slides are then delivered to the veterinary clinical lab where they are stained and analyzed.

The basis for interpretation of smears are the predictable, day-to-day changes in several different cell types found within the vagina during estrus. A single smear is of little value, and to be trusted, a series of daily or every other day smears should be taken.

Embryonic and Fetal Activity

The following discussion of pregnancy is based upon the concept that an "average" mating occurs one day prior to ovulation. Statistical and technical information cited is gleaned from a number of sources, principal of which is "Canine Pregnancy and Parturition," Patrick W. Concannon, *Veterinary Clinics of North America*, May 1986.

Physical union of a sperm cell and an ovum is termed fertilization, and the cell formed by the joining of those two cells is called a *zygote*. Fertilization takes place sometime within a three-day period and occurs about five days after mating. Fertilized ova (zygotes) begin cell division growth, and the growing organisms are then termed *embryos*. The continually dividing and growing embryos travel down the oviducts (see illustration of anatomy of female reproduction tract of female, page 47), heading toward the horns of the uterus. When they reach the uterus they have grown to 32 or 64 cells in size. About the tenth day after mating, the developing embryos move from the oviducts into the uterine horns.

By the second week, the embryonic structures have settled into their places in the uterine horns and are implanted or attached to the walls of the uterus within another day or two. As they implant, and their support membranes (placenta) develop, the embryos are termed *fetuses*.

Golden retriever pups begin their training early.

By the 18th day after mating, placental development is evident. The placenta is made up of a complex of membranous structures surrounding a fetus, connecting it to the dam's uterus by an umbilical cord. It develops with the fetus, and, together with the fluid contained within the membrane sacs, it serves to supply nutrition and protection for the developing fetus.

By the 20th day, uterine swellings are nearly half an inch (12.7 mm) in diameter. They contain both the developing fetuses and their placental tissues. Implantation sites are fairly evenly spaced along the length of either or both horns of the uterus. Implantation does not normally occur in the body of a canine uterus.

Each fetus has its individual placental support structure. Although embryonic and fetal growth is relatively uniform, the varying sizes of fetuses at term confirms the fact that embryos develop independently of one another.

In this discussion, our comments on physical size of the uterus, embryos, and other structures relate to an average-sized animal.

Early Pregnancy Determination

Abdominal palpation is an excellent tool for diagnosing pregnancy, especially in slender, athletic bitches. Many experienced professionals can detect the presence of embryonic structures by the 21st to 25th day of pregnancy. Sometimes we can even count the puppies, although I have lost as many bets as I have won wagering on the exact number that will be born.

Ultrasound imaging of fetuses is sometimes possible as early as 17 days, and is nearly always diagnostic between 21 and 26 days of pregnancy. By the 24th day, ultrasonic evidence of heartbeats may be found. If breeders wish to use ultrasound techniques, the appropriate date for such imaging is about the 25th day after the last breeding. Sometimes, ultrasound at that time will also identify dead fetuses that are being resorbed, a natural phenomenon in canines.

By the 30th day, gross uterine enlargements are slightly over an inch in diameter. At that time they are easily palpated by veterinarians or other trained individuals. X-ray imaging of gravid uteruses may be dangerous and should never be used without justification. When necessary, X-rays should show the soft uterine enlargements by the 30th day as well. Fetal skulls usually are not distinctly discernible in X-rays until about the 45th day; teeth should be visible on X-ray at about the 60th day.

After the 30th day, individual fetuses are more difficult to discern by abdominal palpation. That is due to the increase in placental tissues and fluids, and general enlargement

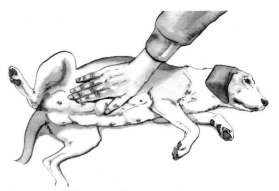

Correct technique to palpate movement of fetuses.

of the uterus. As you would expect, the greatest weight gain in the developing fetuses occurs during the last four weeks of pregnancy.

A word of caution to the novice breeder: If you wish to palpate your pregnant dog's abdomen in order to follow the development of the puppies, take time to learn a safe, reliable technique from a trained professional. Trustworthy, dependable abdominal palpation can't be learned from a book—the technique takes extensive practice and sensitive fingers to become proficient. *Don't endanger your bitch's pregnancy by attempting palpation without detailed, hands-on instruction.*

Fetal Resorption and Abortion

It is generally accepted that a fairly large number of fetuses are resorbed during pregnancy. Research has

An energetic Labrador retriever hits the water with ducks on her mind.

shown resorption of 11 percent to 13 percent of implanted embryos without outward symptoms in the pregnant bitches. Resorption is a natural phenomenon in many species, including canines.

Abortion of individual puppies is also fairly common. Like resorption, it is a natural canine reproduction phenomenon. It is possible for one or two fetuses to be aborted and the rest of the litter to remain implanted in the uterus and delivered normally. Abortions are often undetected, especially in kenneled dogs, because bitches tend to eat the fetus as soon as it is aborted.

Abortion of all fetuses may also occur, accompanied by systemic illness in the bitch. Signs of illness might include appetite loss, fever, depression, and sometimes vomiting. Anytime an entire litter is aborted, or when foul, copious vaginal discharge

is seen, have the dog examined immediately.

The causes for fetal deaths and consequent abortion or resorption are many and varied and beyond the scope of this book. The subject is mentioned primarily to point out that the phenomenon may or may not be accompanied by illness of the bitch. If abortion is seen or suspected, you should make notes of the time and date and the attitude and condition of the bitch. Also record her appetite and temperature twice daily for several days thereafter. If she shows signs of illness, consult your veterinarian immediately.

Hormonal Changes

Progesterone is the dominant hormone expressed during pregnancy. For those readers who appreciate endocrinology (the study of hormones), it is interesting to note that progesterone levels in a pregnant bitch vary little from those of a non-pregnant bitch during diestrus.

Prolactin is a hormone that originates from the pituitary gland and influences mammary development and milk production. The level of prolactin increases considerably during the last half of pregnancy, then surges even higher as progesterone levels decline during the last two or three days of pregnancy (see Chapter 10, Lactation, beginning on page 107).

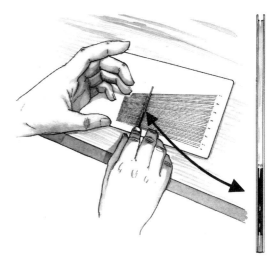

Hematocrit is a quick technique to measure anemia.

Blood Cell Changes

Red blood cells transport oxygen to all tissues and organs of the body, and are thus vital for life. As those cells age and die, their numbers are constantly replenished. A decrease in numbers of red blood cells results in a decrease in the oxygen-carrying capacity of blood, and is one of the causes of anemia. (There are other types and causes of anemia as well.)

In many species, including canines, pregnant females are normally anemic. That sounds like an oxymoron or a conflict of terms. If anemia refers to a deficiency of red blood cells, how can a normal animal be anemic?

The measure of red blood cells, compared to the total blood volume is termed "hematocrit." In a non-pregnant dog, we will consider a normal hematocrit to be approximately 50 percent, meaning that red blood cells constitute 50 percent of the dog's total blood volume. This is an arbitrary figure; some are normally higher or lower.

Pregnant bitches' hematocrits decline to about 40 percent at the time of embryo implantation. They continue to fall, and by the time of whelping, they are typically about 30 percent to 35 percent (sometimes quoted as 29 to 35 percent). That anemic phenomenon is thought to be due to an increase in plasma volume, necessary to support the new life being nurtured within the bitch's body. She accommodates the increased need for blood volume easily, but her red blood cell-producing mechanism doesn't keep up with the rather sudden, temporary increased demand.

Physical and Attitude Changes

Changes seen in a bitch's first pregnancy always seem more dramatic than in subsequent breedings. Depending on the individual involved, a young female's attitude and physical changes may be somewhat startling to her human companions.

Early in gestation, for the first two or three weeks, she will exhibit no appreciable changes in appearance or behavior.

About the fourth week, her appetite begins to increase. She will likely take more naps, but remain playful and energetic for the most part.

The earliest noticeable abdominal enlargement varies with the general conformation and condition of the dog.

By the fourth or fifth week of pregnancy you will probably discern some abdominal distention. It is most apparent in animals with slender builds and short hair, especially when lying on their sides.

By the fifth or sixth week, her play and exercise periods will shorten and her appetite will be notably increased. When viewed from the rear, her abdomen will begin to take on the typical pear shape by the end of the sixth week.

The seventh, eighth, and ninth weeks are the periods of most dramatic change in appearance and attitude. The fetuses grow rapidly, the dam gradually becomes more sedentary, and her appetite response to caloric demand is greatly increased.

Early in that period the fetuses can be observed moving in the dam's abdomen. By laying your flattened palm *gently* on her abdomen while she is lying on her side, you can easily discern the pups' rather energetic activity.

As the ninth week approaches, her mammary development may become obvious, but that feature is not constant. I have known females that show no increase in mammary size until the puppies are born. In others, the glands are filled and milk may even drip from them several days before labor begins. Many times, especially in long-haired breeds, bitches will pull tufts of hair from their abdomens to expose the nipples of each mammary gland.

Another natural variation between individual dogs is their socialization with humans during the last three weeks of pregnancy. Some females, especially house pets, seek the constant companionship of their human family during that period. They follow their owners from room to room, and by the final week of gestation, they begin sleeping beside or in their owners' beds. Others tend to become reclusive and seek a quiet, dark place to hide for hours at a time.

Some near-term pregnant females become so loving they are almost a nuisance. They attempt to sit on laps, beg for petting while you are eating dinner, and refuse to leave their favorite members of the family alone. Others develop the opposite attitude. Especially during the last week of pregnancy, they will act very aloof, and prefer their own company. They will even shun petting and grooming in favor of resting alone.

Irritability

Although it is not common, some individuals become irritable near delivery time. They are less tolerant of small children's noisy play, and sometimes exhibit a tendency to snap. If that occurs, the owner must weigh all the circumstances before disciplinary measures are taken. If the dog showed no irritability until the final few weeks of pregnancy, and then only under special circumstances, the bad attitude will probably resolve itself as soon as her puppies are a couple of weeks old.

If your pregnant dog snaps at a toddler, it is wrong to place all the blame on either the bitch or the youngster. The child should be instructed to give the dog some space. That is difficult for a small child to understand, when only a few weeks ago the animal tolerated the child's attempts to groom or play with her.

At the same time, the dog should be reprimanded verbally. Don't allow her training and human socialization to deteriorate. The best course to take is one of physical separation of

the child and dog except when both are within your reach. Then the child can be allowed to gently pet the dog for a brief time under supervision.

Exercise

Walks and play periods are of great importance throughout gestation. Wrestling and rough play should be discontinued when the bitch is bred, but other types of exercise should be maintained. Animals with good firm muscle tone and minimal body fat experience fewer whelping problems. As you increase your female's diet during pregnancy, be sure she is not storing excess fat (see Pregnancy Nutrition, page 67). Sometimes, due to her attitude change, you may need to insist on regular exercise. Take her for walks, throw a ball for her, or do whatever it takes to keep her in good athletic condition.

Nesting

Common to nearly all bred bitches is a nesting behavior (see Stage I Labor, page 77). It can begin any time during pregnancy, but is usually more visible during the last few days. It gradually becomes more intense and should alert you to prepare for puppies.

When you decided to breed your bitch, you knew that certain physical space requirements were needed. One of them was a quiet

Healthy pug puppies at the take-out counter, waiting for their lunch.

place for whelping and raising puppies. Now is the time to review your plans and prepare for the next phase of dog breeding.

During the last two weeks of pregnancy, you should consider confining your dog to the particular area you plan for her to occupy during delivery and raising her puppies. That place can be any easily accessible room or part of a room. When she is not actually with the family, she should be kept in the special area. Her nesting box should be constructed and kept there, and until whelping time, her usual bedding should be placed in the nesting box (see nesting box discussion beginning on page 79).

False Pregnancy (Pseudocyesis or Pseudopregnancy)

This unique condition is relatively common in canines. It occurs on the same time schedule as normal pregnancy, but there are no puppies involved. It is observed in all ages, and I have personally seen it follow a bitch's first estrus at six or seven months of age. The incidence seems to be much higher in old, unbred bitches than in younger animals.

Bitches in false pregnancy display nesting urges and activities and exhibit similar personality changes to a bitch in normal pregnancy. At the appropriate time for whelping, they often pant, pace, and show signs of abdominal straining identical to normal whelping activities. I have been called to assist in several dystocias when a bitch is straining in what appears to be active phase II labor without producing a puppy. On examination and X-ray, the uterus is proven empty.

Bitches in false pregnancy often develop milk in all mammary glands, although sometimes the fluid resembles serum instead of normal milk. They "adopt" stuffed toys or other inanimate objects, and they clean and attempt to nurse their "adopted" offspring with all the maternal attention of a fine brood bitch. I have known a number of false pregnancy bitches that produced milk and actually nursed orphaned neighborhood kittens or puppies for several weeks.

Treatment of false pregnancy is not usually necessary when the situation corrects itself in a few weeks. The less attention a bitch receives, the quicker her recovery will likely be. If her maternal tendencies can be ignored, do so. If her activities are creating a nuisance, however, mild tranquilization may help relieve the signs of nesting.

Estrogens are sometimes used, and are effective in curtailing the false pregnancy, but in my experience they cause more problems than they correct. I do not recommend using hormones. Before initiating any therapy, be positive that she is not actually pregnant!

Kenneled Bitches

As you may have noticed, the preceding discussion relates to brood bitches that are kept in an owner's home—kennel breeding and housing is quite another situation. Although the same facts apply, the human-dog relationship and interaction is vastly different. When an animal is housed in a kennel with an exercise run, and does not come into extended daily contact with her owners, good breeding management is quite different.

Dogs of all breeds that are raised from puppyhood to and through breeding ages in kennels seem to do very well. Commercial breeding establishments often find the arrangement easier to manage, and many of the country's winning show dogs are kenneled practically all their lives.

Kenneled dogs are less apt to be inadvertently bred by the neighborhood fence jumper and escape into a busy street is less likely. Bitches raised together in kennels usually synchronize their estrous cycles and may be easier to breed. Kenneled stud dogs are often the most predictable sires available.

I have no argument with kennels and the brood stock they house. I believe that kennel owners miss a great deal of the joy and satisfaction of dog ownership in general, but from a dog breeding business standpoint, they are usually quite efficient.

This young Lab's career has been chosen, and training is already underway.

Pregnancy Nutrition

Energy requirements are measured in kilocalories, abbreviated *kcal*. Those calories are the products of metabolism of fats, proteins, carbohydrates, amino acids, and fatty acids. When you see kcal, think of energy and remember this axiom!

Overfeeding bitches during early pregnancy is bad, and underfeeding them in late pregnancy is worse!

Energy Requirements

A pregnant bitch's weight gain is usually negligible during the first three to four weeks of gestation. Energy requirements may increase slightly during those early weeks, but not appreciably until the fourth week. Then there is a linear increase in kcal requirements from four weeks through the ninth week. Midway (4½ weeks) through gestation, her requirements are about 10 percent above maintenance. By the seventh week, her requirements are 30 percent increased, and beginning the eighth week they are about 50 percent increased. At whelping time, her energy requirements are at least 60 percent above maintenance levels, according to the National Research Council (NRC).

Total increases in bitches' body weights during pregnancy vary between 20 and 50 percent. Most of the increase is during the second half of gestation.

The above figures are averages and you may be fooled if you attempt to apply them rigidly. Monitor weight gain by checking at least once a week. The variation between individuals is great. Some pregnant bitches are reported to require as much as 20 percent more kcal, some as much as 20 percent less than the average. Such wide variations are caused by litter size, other energy expenditures, ambient temperature, and stress factors. These variations are a strong recommendation for use of free choice feeding of a premium quality dry dog food, when it is feasible.

Percentage of Fat and Protein

For the sake of comparison, certain numbers should be discussed. Dry food during gestation should contain at least 27 percent protein and 10 percent fat. Canned food should be at least 8 percent protein and 3 percent fat by weight. The smaller numbers in canned foods is due to the water content of the food. If you read canned food labels carefully, you will find that a great deal of its weight (up to 66 percent) is made up of water that provides no fat, protein, or carbohydrate.

Vitamin Supplementation

Vitamin and mineral deficiencies can cause reproductive difficulties in dogs. Micro-nutrient elements, especially fat-soluble vitamins (A, D, E, K), are diminished by heat used in the production of commercial dog foods. Storage causes additional

Children must be taught how to handle their companions properly.

losses. To compensate for those losses, manufacturers include carefully calculated excess amounts of those elements when the food is formulated.

Although not usually necessary, adding vitamins to your bitch's diet is probably not harmful. If you are concerned about adequate vitamins and minerals, ask your veterinarian to suggest a broad spectrum supplement that is designed for use in pregnant or lactating bitches. Be sure to use it strictly according to label instructions because toxicities can be caused by using supplements in excess of the label recommendations.

Calcium Supplements

Calcium deserves separate mention. Breeders are often concerned about calcium in bitches' diets because of eclampsia (see page 117). In my experience, oral calcium supplementation will not prevent eclampsia.

Breeders of giant and large breeds sometimes fear insufficient dietary calcium for bone formation in rapidly maturing fetuses. Prior to the advent of intensive research into canine nutrient requirements, calcium supplementation was necessary in large pregnant bitches' diets, to assure normal skeletal growth in the fetuses.

Today, if excellent quality dog foods are fed, calcium supplementation is not necessary or advised. Adequate levels of calcium are included in virtually all the better quality dog foods. If a need for supplemental calcium has been identified, and you wish to add that mineral to your pregnant bitch's diet, consult a good canine nutrition text before doing so, or discuss the subject with your veterinarian. The balance between vitamin D and calcium is critical.

Micro-nutrients' Toxicity

Excessive supplementation of vitamin A, vitamin D, and iodine may be toxic to your dog. You can easily cause problems by over-supplementing your animal's diet with those elements and you can cause dangerous imbalances by supplementing her diet with zinc and copper as well.

Home-made Diets

As previously discussed (see Home-made Diets, page 27), it is possible to formulate a kitchen diet that will support a pregnant bitch. However, I believe few people are equipped or qualified to do so without training. If you fear the preservatives in commercially manufactured diets, or if you simply wish to cook for your dog, please don't start mixing and cooking without adequate information.

- Beware of health food store recipes.
- Stay away from vegetarian diets.
- Locate recent data that has been formulated specifically for pregnant bitches
- Do not deviate from the ingredient list or the recipe.

Drugs during Pregnancy

Anything that is absorbed from the intestine or injected into a pregnant bitch can affect the fetuses. Dietary changes, oral medications, or injected antibiotics can pass the placental barrier and enter unborn puppies. Fetuses are subjected to the effects of almost any product given to the dam.

It is not my intention to discuss here the mechanism by which substances are transferred through the placenta, but only to make you aware that it happens, and warn you of certain commonly used products that can cause trouble.

Anesthesia

Anesthetizing a pregnant bitch should be avoided whenever possible; however, if it becomes necessary, your veterinarian will know the safest product to use. If the bitch is in the first few weeks of gestation, be sure to tell the clinician, because early pregnancy is not outwardly obvious. I practiced in an area where porcupines were so numerous they constituted a nuisance and we often anesthetized three or four dogs a day to remove quills. On many occasions, we administered short-acting anesthetics to pregnant bitches without disturbing pregnancy or causing fetal problems.

Other Drugs

Aspirin and other nonsteroidal antiinflammatory drugs are known to cross the placental barrier and can cause major problems in fetuses. Large doses of several vitamins, notably A and D, can cause fetal problems. Some tranquilizers can be very dangerous, as are diuretics and sulfas.

Many breeders use over-the-counter antibiotics in their animals for various infectious conditions. In proper doses, antibiotics of the penicillin family are relatively safe to use in pregnant bitches. Tetracycline and many other broad spectrum antibiotics should *never* be given. Streptomycin (often used in combination with penicillin) can cause kidney or ear problems in fetuses, and should be avoided. *Before using any antibiotic, either orally or by injection, check with your veterinarian.*

Steroids such as hydrocortisone and prednisone are often administered to dogs with allergies or

The first stage of a lifetime companionship.

Caution: Drugs of any kind, used for any purpose, must be administered cautiously. Before giving your pregnant bitch anything other than her food, water, and approved supplements, confer with your veterinarian and evaluate the risk to the fetuses.

Pregnancy Termination

There are sometimes unfortunate situations in which a bitch is inadvertently bred, and it is desirable to terminate her pregnancy. Perhaps a purebred bitch escaped from her kennel or your yard, or a planned mating proved to be a mistake after the fact, for example, if it is discovered after mating that the male carries some unwanted genetic feature. Termination of pregnancy of a pet that you never intended bred is another possible reason for pregnancy termination and may be appropriately handled by surgical intervention early in pregnancy.

Spaying: Spaying a pregnant bitch as soon as her outward signs of estrus disappear does not pose a high risk in the hands of an experienced surgeon.

If your plans include spaying your pet anyway, and she is accidentally bred, this may be the time. Scheduling the surgery at the appropriate time of gestation is critically important—call your veterinarian as soon as the accidental breeding occurs. In pet dogs that are not intended for

asthma. Those and other antiinflammatory steroids (especially dexamethasone), can cause abortion or anomalies in developing fetuses.

Epileptic animals often require daily doses of anticonvulsant drugs such as phenobarbital, primidone, and others. Consult with your veterinarian about continuing those medications during pregnancy. It may be more prudent to maintain the anticonvulsant drug dosage and risk puppy anomalies than to risk the bitch's life by discontinuing the drug. Each case must be evaluated according to known and predictable factors.

70

breeding purposes, I believe that early spaying is the best pregnancy termination choice.

Estrogen administration. Some breeders and veterinarians continue to use estrogen to terminate an unwanted pregnancy. Most commonly, estradiol is given during estrus or early diestrus, as soon as possible after a known mismating. That means the drug may be used to abort a bitch before she is positively known to be pregnant.

In the author's experience, risks associated with estrogenic hormones do not support their use. Typically, a treated female exhibits prolonged estrus, sometime several weeks, during which she may continually stand for breeding. Repeated breedings certainly enhance the possibility of uterine infection.

Pyometra, one of the most dangerous types of uterine infection, is documented in up to 25 percent of estradiol-treated females. Many other undesirable side effects of estrogen use have been reported, including future erratic estrous cycling, persistent estrus, and aplastic anemia. It may also promote the growth of preexisting mammary tumors.

Prostaglandin. Removal of the progesterone source in a pregnant bitch will cause the placenta to be unsupported, and will result in abortion. This concept is applied in another abortive technique. Prostaglandin is a hormone-like element originally derived from male prostate glands. To cause abortion, it is given by injection, two or three times daily for four consecutive days during diestrus.

The treatment regimen usually also involves a pre-treatment serum progesterone level determination and vaginal smear evaluation. The series of prostaglandin injections are sometimes followed by an injection of progesterone. Ultrasound imaging can be used to confirm that the embryos are resorbed. Recent studies of prostaglandin use have shown complete embryo resorption even after the time of positive pregnancy determination. Side effects of the injections are usually mild and include excess salivation, panting, and sometimes vomiting. Prostaglandin injections should only be given by a veterinarian who is experienced in their use. I have great confidence in the efficacy and safety of the technique when used by experts.

Anti-progesterone. Another possibility for safe abortion of a bitch is administration of an anti-progestin drug. Such a drug causes resorption of the embryos, and may pose low, acceptable risk potential. The commercial availability of anti-progestin products is limited and expensive, as of this writing. Ask your veterinarian for further information, since new technology continually develops.

Pyometra

Pyometra is a specific type of metritis (see pages 119–120) in which there is little or no visible vaginal discharge. It is a diestrus disease that is interrelated to pregnancy. Academically, four types of pyometra are described in veterinary literature, the first two of which rarely create any significant health risk. In all four, the uterus fills with fluids, but in types I and II, the uncontaminated condition resolves itself without presence of bacterial infection. Type IV is a chronic infectious condition, creating long-term signs of illness in the affected bitch. It is difficult to diagnose without laboratory testing.

Symptoms

Type III is the pyometra commonly presented to veterinary clinicians as an emergency. In the author's experience, the clinical illness suddenly alarms owners within the first month after estrus. Sometimes the early symptoms of lethargy and depression are believed by owners to be associated with pregnancy until the animal becomes toxic and obviously sick. There is typically no visible vaginal discharge in many cases of pyometra, which makes it easier to go unnoticed. There may be some abdominal distension that may be mistaken for normal pregnancy as well.

The disease progresses rapidly, and when advanced symptoms appear and the bitch's appetite ceases, owners begin to watch her more closely. Vomiting, disorientation, and dehydration call attention to the seriousness of the disease.

Pyometra is often associated with increased progesterone hormone levels and their effect on the lining of the uterus. Naturally, there is a bacterial component to the disease as well. It probably gains entrance into the uterus via the normal genital tract during estrus.

Causes

During the years when progesterone heat-prevention products were promoted and marketed, pyometra was one of the most commonly diagnosed intact bitch diseases in our practice. The progesterone used in both injectable and oral birth control products unquestionably was associated with pyometra. Long after most veterinarians stopped using those products, we continued seeing pyometra in non-cycling bitches that had been subjected to those progesterone products.

A current, more relative potential cause of pyometra is the use of "mismating" estrogen drugs. They are often called "morning after" shots by owners, and when administered subsequent to unplanned matings, they interfere with normal pregnancy processes. Following an injection, standing heat is often prolonged for two or three weeks, and sometimes owners allow the bitches to be repeatedly bred. The drug alone may somehow promote pyometra, or perhaps the extended estrus may be involved. Whatever the technical cause, in my experi-

ence, estrogens used to prevent normal pregnancy result in a high incidence of pyometra.

Treatment

Pyometra is sometimes successfully treated medically with prostaglandin (combined with antibiotic and fluid therapy) but the jury is still out on the success rate for returning a bitch to a normal breeding status. I caution breeders to only consider medical treatment for pyometra if the bitch's reproductive value equals the value of her life. Conservative medical treatment is often very expensive and without guarantees. It has earned a place in our discussion, but is not standardized well enough for this author to recommend it without reservation.

In my experience, all diagnosed cases of pyometra are candidates for extensive intravenous fluid and antibiotic support, accompanied by immediate surgical ovariohysterectomy.

Bernese mountain dogs were bred for pulling carts, and like most dogs, they love to stay busy.

Chapter 7
Whelping

In canine breeding terminology, when a bitch delivers her puppies, the process is called *whelping.* Dog breeders need to be aware of the signs that accompany normal whelping, the stages of labor, and delivery itself. The whelping process is exciting to watch, but it usually doesn't require your help.

Too Much Help

Example: Fresh out of college, many years ago, I had an opportunity to consult with an owner of a bitch that abandoned her litter. According to the initial history provided, the setter delivered her very first litter of nine normal, live puppies but, immediately after delivery, she refused to nurse them or care for them in any way. After an hour spent examining the bitch and hungry puppies, searching for some maternal health problem, the cause for abandonment was revealed.

It seems the owner, anxious to minimize stress on her wonderful pet, took each puppy from the dam as it was born. She carefully dried and massaged the pups, properly separated and disinfected the umbilical cords, and destroyed the placentas. The puppies were placed in a warm box and their meconium excretions were carefully cleaned up as soon as they were passed. After all pups were born, the dam's genital area was thoroughly washed with soap and water, and she was united with her puppies. The dam got up, put her nose in the air, left the area, and proceeded to ignore her maternal duties.

Following my advice, for a few days she was held down four or five times a day for the puppies to nurse. My primary concern was to supply colostrum to the pups, but I also hoped she would reconsider and adopt them. When that chore became too time-consuming, the family resigned themselves to bottle-feeding the litter. The puppies lived and seven weeks later were sold, but without the usual mother-bonding. Needless to say, the owner was not particularly happy with her self-inflicted, seven-week-long responsibilities.

Now the good news: The next time the bitch was bred the owner took a seat in the audience and the dam cheerfully delivered, cleaned, and raised her family without help. I have had other similar experiences, but none that involved such a complete, irreversible abandonment attitude.

Some respected, professional dog breeders routinely employ a philosophy similar to the above scenario, and seem to get away with it. I suspect they probably buy a lot of milk replacer and nursing bottles. I know a few of them also have their veterinarian on alert because they have an inordinate need for cesarean section deliveries. I believe there is sometimes a connection between cesarean sections and unwarranted human participation in whelping.

I don't subscribe to the concept and practice of taking over the dam's responsibilities. I believe it reduces natural, instinctive canine maternal behavior. I wonder if it may eventually produce a bloodline of maternal invalids? My experience indicates that if you are determined to do most of the dam's work for her, you must start with a terribly tolerant bitch. Then stand ready to accept total responsibility for the puppies, since her interest in her offspring will certainly wane.

I suggest that our help should be reserved for those times when a puppy or the dam is at risk. As an owner and breeder, you have the responsibility to oversee your dog's whelping, and to render assistance when and if needed. To prepare for that eventuality, you must predict the approximate whelping date, recognize the elements of a normal delivery, be alerted to potential problems, have the knowledge necessary to assist, and have certain equipment and facilities ready.

Predicting Whelping Time

If a mating is unplanned and the exact breeding date is uncertain, whelping time may be difficult to determine.

One of the most time-honored and successful dog breeding techniques is to mate a bitch on the first day she stands for a male, then every other day until she will no longer receive him. When such intentional breeding includes several matings over a period of a week, the exact whelping date may be unpredictable. Even in a single supervised breeding, without knowing a bitch's exact ovulation date there is a great range of possible whelping dates.

When pregnancy is suspected, but you are unsure of the date your dog was bred, your veterinarian may estimate the breeding and whelping dates by examining the female. A professional examination consists of associating your history of the bitch's heat cycle with careful palpation of her abdomen. To be effective and accurate, an examination should be done shortly after the outward signs of estrus have passed, and repeated every four days for two or three exams.

In some instances, a health care professional may also suggest using hormone assays, ultrasound imaging, and, if justified, X-rays, to assist in determining whelping dates. In most normal pregnancies, the costs of laboratory tests and examinations preclude their use. In early pregnancy, a history review, and physical examination, including abdominal palpation, is often a reasonable and acceptable alternative.

Imminent Whelping Signs

In late pregnancy, when no other information is available, a litter's estimated time of arrival may be roughly calculated by observation of the expectant mother. It is therefore important to recognize the earliest signs of labor and parturition. Be aware that no outward signs are constant or predictable in all females. Your bitch may exhibit one, some, all, or none of the following signs. Magnitude and duration of all signs are relative as well. An athletic young cocker carrying two puppies will likely exhibit less pronounced physical signs than a six-year-old Labrador carrying her third litter of ten puppies.

Several days before labor begins, pregnant females' appetites gradually diminish. They become restless and sedentary. Belly muscles relax and abdomens become more pendulous and distended. The fetuses' activities are less pronounced, and the dams' mammary glands begin to enlarge. Milk production is not a trustworthy indicator by itself. I have known bitches to produce milk two weeks in advance of parturition, and others that produce no milk until several hours after whelping.

One routinely observed sign of impending parturition is relaxation of the vulva and pelvic musculature. Tissue surrounding the vulva becomes flaccid and pendulous.

A sure sign that uterine labor contractions have begun is the presence of a green vaginal discharge. It is the result of early uterine placental detachment and may be seen several hours before a bitch produces her first pup. The green fluid, called *lochia,* is intermittently observed until several days or a week after whelping.

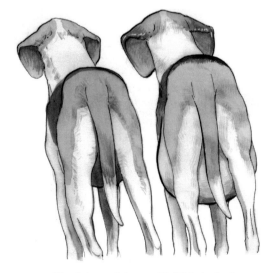

Pendulous abdomen (right) is typical as parturition nears.

Body Temperature

The most predictable, nearly constant indicator of imminent whelping is a female's body temperature. Hypothermia, or decrease in body temperature, lags behind the decline of serum progesterone hormones by 12 to 24 hours. Normally, the temperature drops several degrees, from a normal of 101.5°F (38.6°C) to less than 100°F (37.7°C), often as low as 98°F (36.6°C) or 99°F (37.2°C). This happens about 12 to 24 hours before productive Stage II labor begins.

If you decide to take her temperature, follow a specific routine. Use a lubricated oral stubby human thermometer. Insert the bulb end into her rectum about one inch (2.5 cm) and hold it there for a minute or two. Repeat the procedure three times a day, and record the time and temperature on a note pad. To be a valid predictor, the temperature must be taken and recorded at the same times each day. A random, hit or miss technique is not of much value in predicting whelping time because the normal body temperature rises and falls slightly with exercise, rest, and meals.

Stage I Labor

Stage I labor refers to the period of nesting behavior during which time there are uterine contractions, but active, voluntary abdominal contractions have not yet begun. These signs should alert you to begin serious preparations for puppies.

After the bitch's temperature drops and her appetite diminishes or ceases, she will start acting strangely. She may show various nesting signs for a week or more before whelping, but at this time they become intense. A typical pregnant bitch will choose a spot where she plans to have her litter. It may be in a closet, under or on a bed, behind a sofa, or any other place that seems appropriate to her at the time.

Once a nest site is chosen, she scratches and digs at its floor, turns around several times, lies down, gets up, and repeats the performance. She frequently returns to the same spot and repeats her nesting activities each time.

When she begins panting, pacing about restlessly, sometimes whining,

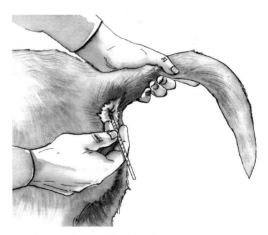

Most essential tool for breeders is a thermometer.

and often demanding attention from her favorite family members, time is short.

Until you become familiar with your dog's whelping behavioral pattern, general nesting activities are warning signals, but are not critical signs of the particular whelping time. For future reference, I suggest that you keep daily notes on a permanent calendar relative to her activities, appetite, and attitude. Those notes with the actual delivery time and date will be invaluable in interpreting and predicting whelping times of future litters.

As labor progresses, the female's panting is more constant and pronounced as she displays other signs of nonspecific discomfort. Frequently licking her genitalia, she stands up, turns around, digs with her forefeet, lies down, then gets up again. She is obviously nervous and uncomfortable.

At this time, you may notice a clear, odorless, stringy vaginal discharge, appearing much like raw egg white. It is the mucus plug that filled her cervix during pregnancy, and escapes at the time of cervical dilation. When you see that, keep her under close observation if you want to watch the whelping process.

Stage II Labor

Finally, as whelping time approaches and productive Stage II labor begins, the expectant female lies on her side and begins to strain. Some whelping bitches assume a squatting position in early hard labor, and appear to be straining to urinate or defecate.

Her vulva continues to swell and dilate, and it becomes more flaccid, as a moderate quantity of clear, straw-colored or light pink fluid leaks from the birth canal. Uterine contractions intensify, and external abdominal muscular contractions are very apparent to an observant owner. The combination of uterine and abdominal contractions press the puppy from the horn of the uterus through the cervix, the vagina, and into the outside world.

Puppies are delivered from the uterine horns in an alternating manner, usually beginning with the horn containing the most fetuses.

Stage II labor may continue from an hour or two in very small litters to 24 hours. If it persists for four hours or more without the birth of a puppy, call your veterinarian (see Chapter 8, Dystocia, beginning on page 87). There are no standard time schedules applicable to the duration of whelping activities. Most deliveries are completed in four to six hours. Often, the observable labor signs last longer for the first puppy delivery than for those that come later. Likewise, the time between the first and second puppies is often longer than the interval between the later deliveries.

Puppies often make their appearance in pairs. Two will be delivered in rapid succession, with a longer time span between them and the next pup.

Preparation for Whelping

When the signs of impending labor are seen, or better yet, at about eight weeks gestation, confine your bitch to the place you have chosen for her to whelp. Visit her often and spend as much time with her as possible. Most dogs appreciate their owners' comforting voices and touch at this time, but many will resent the intrusion of strangers. If whelping a tiny dog within the confines of a kennel or playpen, leave it in a quiet place; don't carry it from room to room. All dogs prefer stable, quiet seclusion at the time of whelping.

Between deliveries, a bitch may whine to go outside. Let her out into the yard to relieve herself as often as necessary, *but only under close observation*. That is particularly important if she is whelping at night, and is critical in inclement weather. Unsupervised trips into the backyard may cause you to lose a puppy that was dropped in a snowbank or under a bush.

If you don't confine her to a secluded place containing a nesting box, she will probably seek out her own whelping place that is quiet and out of the family traffic pattern. She will spend much of her last few days of pregnancy in her chosen nest, which may not always be acceptable to you, especially if it is on your bed, on the living room sofa, or on your white carpet behind a piece of furniture.

Bitches often choose inappropriate place to whelp.

Whelping is a messy business. There will be several ounces of clear, yellow-pink placental fluid expelled with each puppy, as well as some blood and thick greenish-black fluid. Those colorful fluids will soil her coat and leave permanent stains on carpet and furniture. They are difficult, if not impossible, to remove from painted surfaces and may even etch vinyl floor tile.

If your dog is long-haired and you have not previously done so, carefully clip the long hair from her anal and vulvar region, and from the lower side of her tail prior to whelping.

Nesting and Whelping Box

A nesting or whelping box need be nothing more than a sturdy cardboard box that is large enough to accommodate the bitch when she is fully stretched out. Its sides should be high enough to contain her litter of active puppies for the

Bumper rail inside whelping box protects puppies from smothering, especially in large and giant breeds.

first two or three weeks of life, but low enough so she can easily enter without abrading her full, protruding mammary glands. The advantage of using a cardboard box is obvious— it can be discarded and replaced, cost free, at any time.

In toy breeds, fiberglass dog carriers are often used as nesting boxes. Sometimes the top portion of plastic airline carriers are removed, and the bottom portion serves the purpose quite well.

Professional breeders often have specially constructed whelping or nesting boxes. That is particularly important when raising large and giant breeds. Construction is usually of plywood, and is designed to accommodate the brood bitch fully stretched out. It has a bumper rail around the inside of the box to protect the puppies from being smothered or squashed by the dam. The bumper rail should be wide enough to allow a puppy's body to fit comfortably under it. The rail's height from the box floor should be sufficient to accommodate a puppy, but

low enough so the dam's foot or rump won't reach the pup as she enters, leaves, sits, and lies down in the box.

A whelping box with bumper rail is an excellent idea, even in small breeds, but in giants and large breeds it is critical.

Building a Whelping/Nesting Box

Our malamute whelping box was constructed from ¾-inch (2 cm) thick marine plywood, to withstand washing better. It was four feet by six feet (1.22 m by 1.82 m) and the sides were 12 inches (77 cm) high. We used countersunk brass screws in its construction.

Inside the box, on all four sides, was a rail elevated from the floor. The rail was made of a two-inch by six-inch (5 cm by 15 cm) board, fastened to the box's sides, and extending six inches (15 cm) into the box. The height of the rail was adjustable from about three inches (7.6 cm) off the floor to about six inches (15 cm). This allowed us to set it low when the puppies were first born, and elevate it as the puppies grew. The rail was removed when the puppies were about four weeks old.

We trimmed the inside joints and corners of the box with mitered ¾-inch (2 cm) hardwood base cove that was glued in place with waterproof contact cement. The box was finished inside and out with several coats of marine urethane varnish.

Chihuahuas don't seem to realize they are the world's smallest dogs.

The box was very durable, easily cleaned, and lasted through years of use without repair or problem. The marine finish resisted stains very well and the box was easily disinfected before and after each use. Its only drawback was storage when not in use.

If you are serious about breeding dogs, invest in the material and labor necessary to construct a good nesting box, especially if you are raising large dogs. Obviously, the size of the box is adjusted to the size of your breed.

Alternatives. If your bitch is reluctant to adapt to a nesting box, confine her to a room where no other comfortable bed is available. For large or giant breeds, confinement to a garage might be appropriate—but only if it is clean, dry, and kept at normal room temperature.

Many breeders of toys and terriers use portable nylon net or plastic baby playpens to confine their

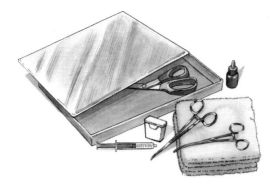

Whelping supplies to have ready:
Stack of clean, dry washcloths, Hemostat
forceps, Dental floss, 3 cc syringe without
needle, Scissors, Bottle of povidone iodine,
Metal pan to boil forceps and scissors

whelping females. The playpens are easily cleaned and are sufficiently large to allow the use of a small kennel or cardboard box as a nesting and whelping box.

An expectant female should be kept confined to the maternity room or kennel all of the time you are unable to observe her, at night, or when you are away from home.

Bedding. Initially, nesting box bedding should be something comfortable like a blanket or towels. When Stage I labor begins and she is obviously serious about whelping, remove all bedding and substitute a dozen layers of flat newspaper. Fresh, flat newspaper is relatively sterile, it absorbs fluids, it can be changed as often as necessary, and puppies are not apt to get lost or tangled up in it.

Bedding that is soft and loose allows puppies to tunnel into folds, where they can be smothered or

stepped on by the dam. Whelping box bedding of foam will be torn up by the bitch, soaked, and ruined with fluid stains. Don't whelp or raise puppies on foam. They can nurse on its fragments and corners, and it is dangerous if swallowed.

Whelping Supplies

When whelping begins, find a comfortable vantage point from which to observe. Rarely will your assistance be required, but just in case, before you settle into your chair, check your inventory of supplies. You should have:

- several clean, dry, small terry-cloth towels or wash cloths
- three or four pairs of boiled hemostat forceps
- a clean plastic two- or three-cc syringe
- a pair of straight, blunt-tipped surgical scissors
- a spool of dental floss
- a tube of water-soluble lubricating jelly and small bottle of organic, povidone iodine solution (not scrub soap), which can be purchased at a pharmacy. Pour an ounce of the iodine solution into a wide-mouthed glass vessel such as a baby food jar or a shotglass.

The syringe, hemostat forceps, and scissors may be purchased in pet supply stores or at swap meets. To sterilize them, immerse them in boiling water in a covered pan for 15 minutes. Then pour off the water and let them dry and cool in the covered pan until they are needed.

When the female approaches productive Stage II labor, she will begin to strain, licking at her vulva, and licking up the fluid as it is expelled from the uterus. You will be amazed at how the animal seems to know exactly what to do and how to do it.

The Delivery

Immediately before the first puppy emerges, an opaque bubble of placenta (amniotic sac) will protrude from the dam's vulva. In a retriever-size bitch, it starts out marble size, then golf ball size, and gradually enlarges. The bubble is filled with fluid, and within a few minutes, the puppy's head and front feet are visible within the bubble. At that time, the female may lick and chew at the membranes, tearing them from the pup's face. Then, with a final abdominal contraction, the puppy is forced from the birth canal. The entire placental sac usually follows each puppy from the uterus, and remains attached to the puppy via the umbilical cord. The placenta may not emerge until shortly before the next puppy is born. Watch for it to be expelled later, if it does not accompany the puppy.

The mother continues licking the puppy, rolling it over and over, cleaning all the blood, meconium (see Glossary, page 172), and pla-

Fluid-filled amniotic sac is the first visible evidence of a puppy's birth.

cental debris from its body. While she is thus cleaning the puppy, she chews the umbilical cord in two, and frequently she consumes the placental tissue.

Eating Placenta

Eating the placenta is a normal, instinctive canine act. Some believe the dam receives great benefit from

Dam sorts and cleans puppies frequently for the first week.

Dam tears amniotic sac from puppy immediately.

the placental fluids. I know breeders who claim dams that consume every placenta have earlier, more copious milk production, and more complete and earlier uterine emptying. Some even insist that placental eating causes the remaining puppies in each litter to be delivered faster and with fewer complications. I doubt those statements are confirmed by research, but neither can I argue with them.

The dam often vomits some of the placental tissues later. Consumed placenta also contributes to her greasy, black and green stools for a day after whelping, but I have not observed illnesses related to either the brief vomiting or dark stools. I believe no particular health benefit or advantage can be attached to placenta eating, but neither does it adversely affect a bitch's health.

I would far rather see a bitch allowed to eat all placental tissues than to see someone interfere with her normal maternal processes by grasping the placentas from her reach and taking them from her. Moderation is the key. If the whelping process allows you to retrieve and destroy some of the placentas, you will see less of the undesirable side effects. But use discretion. *Don't interfere!* Let the dam's natural, maternal instincts prevail.

Resumption of Labor

After a period of ten minutes to an hour of rest, the mother returns to her whelping position and once again abdominal muscular contractions begin. The process is repeated with each puppy until they are all delivered.

Normal Variations

All dogs are individuals with independent, natural tendencies. Don't be alarmed by variations from the described process if labor signs are progressive, if the mother remains alert, and the puppies are born alive and active.

Example: I knew a wonderful black Labrador retriever brood bitch that displayed a very unique whelping style. She delivered a puppy, cleaned it, ate the afterbirth (placenta), nursed the puppy, then insisted on going outside. She took a stroll, urinated, and returned to the house. She munched a bit of dry food, had a drink of water, greeted anyone present, and returned to her whelping box. She checked each of her puppies, rolling them about for a few minutes, then began labor again. That unorthodox procedure was repeated with every puppy.

Normal parturition for that dog lasted from 8 to 24 nail-biting hours, but despite our nervousness, not one puppy was born weak or dead.

While typical pacing, panting, and digging signs accompany most terminal canine pregnancies, I have known dogs that exhibited none of those signs.

- This variation is especially common in experienced bitches with their third or fourth litters. They become more reclusive than usual, and when the time comes, they deliver their puppies, without warning or fanfare, often in the middle of their owners' bed or in some other inappropriate place.
- Many bitches, especially larger breeds, don't lose their appetite. They may have a snack within minutes before whelping, and sometimes even between puppies.
- Once in a while, instead of seeking owner attention, a female will escape from the house and hide out. She may find a whelping place in a shed, under a porch, or on a patio lawn chair. For her safety and the well-being of the puppies, keep your female confined, especially at the calculated delivery time.
- I have known a few females that do not tolerate even their well-loved owners in their whelping area. They seem to postpone active labor until they are quite

The Great Dane is one of the world's largest breeds, and this big fellow outweighs his boy considerably.

alone. If your dog does not move from one stage of labor to the next in a smooth, progressive manner, leave the room and post yourself outside where you can observe through a crack in the door.
- Most puppies arrive into the world head first. Posterior presentations, that is, the tail and hind feet emerging first, are also normal in the canine. In fact, about 40 percent of all puppies are born hind legs first.
- Breech presentations, in which only the tail is presented, may progress normally, or they may be a major cause of concern (see Chapter 8, Dystocia, beginning on page 87).

Expected Duration of Whelping

Schedules are rarely followed. Normal whelping time is related to individual animals. If delivery is progressive, the puppies are born alive and squirming, and the mother is taking good care of them, leave them alone! Don't be alarmed by the duration of rest period between puppies. Normal timing is not defined with a stopwatch—it is an independent, animal-specific period that cannot be predicted. Nevertheless, it is important to watch the whelping process closely and make notes of the timing of whelping events.

Litter Size

The biggest litter I ever saw was 16, but Concannon reports the range of puppies in a litter from 1 to 23. Generally, smaller dogs have smaller litters, but in practice that doesn't always hold true. My miniature schnauzer delivered ten fat, healthy pups and weighed more when she weaned them than when she was bred. Average litter-size data for individual breeds is usually available from breed clubs. Hunting dogs often produce larger litters, and it isn't uncommon to see ten Labs or setter puppies in a litter. Large litters are also common in scent hounds, but our 100-pound Alaskan malamutes usually pro-duced less than six. Pomeranians usually average two or three pups, and many teacup-sized toy breed bitches routinely have only one. Litter size seems to vary among bloodlines within breeds as well. When asked by clients how many puppies a bitch would deliver, I always answer, "All of them, I hope."

When to Call for Help

Keep complete and accurate records. Make notes of the times when nesting begins, appetite diminishes, temperature drops, panting starts, abdominal straining is observed, and when each puppy is born. If hard abdominal labor lasts for more than one hour without the delivery of a puppy, call your veterinarian for advice. That is also very important if you suspect there are more puppies to come, and she stops labor for more than four hours.

In order to give good advice, your health care professional needs as many facts as you can offer. Therefore, your notes on the events leading up to your telephone call are critical. If the bitch whelped previously, notes on that whelping are quite important as well. Above all, if something doesn't seem right to you, don't hesitate to call your veterinarian for advice.

Chapter 8
Dystocia (Difficult Birth)

Dystocia might be defined as any situation in which parturition does not begin, proceed, and conclude in a normal, progressive fashion. It pertains to delay of Stage II labor, prolonged, difficult, or abnormal labor, and many more specific problems. *All dystocias must be treated as emergencies.*

Canine dystocia is not common in active, mature, healthy bitches. However, very old bitches (past six or seven years) and immature females (under a year) have higher incidence of dystocia. Difficult births are also often seen in certain specific breeds (see discussion of certain breed predisposition to dystocia, page 90), or in those that are suffering from poor nutrition, pelvic abnormalities, or diseases.

Before deciding to assist a delivery, be sure that dystocia actually exists. There is a fine line separating true dystocias that require assistance from normal variations in natural whelping processes. To interfere with normal deliveries is a serious mistake, the results of which might have lasting and undesirable consequences.

Interruption of Labor

If labor begins, but is interrupted for some reason, the life of a puppy, the entire litter, and sometimes the bitch, may depend on your recognition of dystocia. Even if you can't or won't physically assist a delivery, your ability to identify a problem and make an early phone call will save lives. If you can assist in the whelping process when appropriate, your chances of a safe, smooth delivery are enhanced. Some dystocias are easily remedied by a knowledgeable breeder; others require professional treatment. Often the best assistance you can render is to call your veterinarian for specific advice about an immediate problem.

Maternal Causes for Dystocia

Delayed or interrupted parturition can have fetal or maternal origin. Maternal dystocias are those related to under-sized birth canals due to bitches' immaturity, or to previous pelvic fractures. Uterine

Keep whelping area quiet.

torsion (twisting) is a rare maternal cause, and primary uterine inertia is another infrequent cause.

I also recognize another type of maternal dystocia. Admittedly, it is not well documented in current veterinary literature, but I am compelled to mention it in passing. It seems to be induced by commotion and disturbance in the whelping area. In those cases, ill-advised owners bring children and sometimes neighbors in to watch their pet whelp. Without thinking, they laugh, cry, talk, point, and generally create a noisy, carnival atmosphere of confusion. Parents hand newborn puppies to children to look at and pet. A four-year-old picks up and quickly drops a wriggling puppy with its bloody, sticky placenta still attached. Family members interfere with the bitch's puppy-cleaning process. These activities are all disruptive to the whelping process and should be discouraged!

A veterinarian is consulted when labor stops. On examination of the dam, no abnormalities are found. Sometimes labor is resumed in response to a hormone injection. Other times, that doesn't work and a cesarean section is necessary.

From a technical, physiological standpoint, it should be impossible for bitches to arbitrarily stop labor once it begins. When uterine contractions start, bitches shouldn't be able to turn the process off, but, in my experience, it happens, and I offer no explanation.

Uterine Inertia

Primary uterine inertia refers to dystocias wherein the nesting phase of Stage I labor progresses, a dam's temperature drops, she shows signs of being ready for Stage II productive labor to begin, but nothing happens. Causes for primary uterine inertia often go undetected. For whatever reason, the dam's uterine and abdominal muscular contractions are not strong enough to effectively initiate normal parturition.

Diagnosis of primary uterine inertia can't be based on your calculation of a 63-day whelping date from your record of a breeding date. Often, presumptive diagnosis is made when no puppies are produced within 24 hours after a bitch's

Do you believe the mischievous innocence expressed in these Lab puppies' faces?

temperature dropped. Should you suspect the condition, call your veterinarian.

Treatment can be medical or surgical. A technique called feathering is sometimes employed. It involves gentle digital massage of the roof of the vagina and should only be attempted by a veterinarian or by someone who has been adequately instructed.

Another possible treatment is administration of a series of posterior pituitary hormone injections. Again, this must be performed by a professional, as improper schedule or incorrect doses of pituitary hormone can have disastrous results.

Intravenous calcium solutions are sometimes helpful in stimulating uterine contractions and overcoming primary uterine inertia. Calcium injections can be fatal if the patient is not closely monitored and the solution is inappropriately used; therefore, I suggest you leave calcium administration to your veterinarian.

Birth canal obstructions may be mistaken for inertia; therefore, neither hormones nor calcium should be administered until the bitch is examined and physical causes for dystocia have been explored and eliminated. If conservative therapy is not successful, cesarean section should be performed as soon as possible.

Uterine Fatigue

Secondary uterine inertia, which I prefer to call uterine fatigue, may result from extended labor due to a large litter. More common in older dams than in young animals, it may also occur when prompt attention is not given to a breech presentation, and excessive energy is expended

Newfoundlands are giants that make wonderful family pets, especially if you have lots of room.

by the bitch. Any fetal or maternal dystocia that is not quickly and effectively corrected may result in uterine fatigue.

Treatment depends first on successfully correcting the cause. Pituitary hormone or calcium may help, but some fatigue cases are resistant to medical therapy and are relieved only by cesarean section.

Uterine Torsion

The rare dystocia known as uterine torsion is a diagnostic and surgical challenge. It occurs when a gravid uterus (filled with fetuses) twists upon itself, thereby blocking normal fetal passage from the uterine horns into the birth canal. Tor-

sion may be suspected and tentatively diagnosed by X-ray films or ultrasound imaging, but its diagnosis is confirmed by laparotomy (exploratory surgery). When torsion exists, both dam and puppies are at risk. A cesarean section is usually performed, and sometimes a hysterectomy is necessary if uterine damage is extensive.

Fetal Dystocia

Fetal dystocia is most commonly caused by abnormally large-sized puppies or fetal monsters. Breed conformation is another common cause of fetal dystocia. The best examples are the disproportionately large heads of English bulldogs, but other brachycephalic breeds (breeds with short, broad heads, usually accompanied by undershot jaws) are predisposed to fetal dystocia as well. The dam's slim hips and narrow pelvis compared to her puppies' wide heads, broad shoulders and chests result in a combination maternal and fetal dystocia potential (cephalopelvic dystocia).

Other fetal dystocias are experienced with some breech presentations. Dead puppies occasionally cause dystocia when they aren't accompanied by adequate placental fluid. Absence of fluid lubrication can cause dystocia even in normal-sized pups.

Although fetal dystocias are sometimes relieved by manipulation and instrumentation, cesarean sections are often the only practical methods of treatment.

When to Call for Help

- As a rule of thumb, when Stage II labor signs are seen, including serious abdominal contractions and placental membranes and fluid appearing from the vulva, a puppy should be delivered within four hours. Typically the time will be much shorter, but if 4 hours have elapsed without a puppy born, it is time to call for help.
- If a puppy's nose is presented and visible at the vulva and no delivery progress is made for 10 or 15 minutes, call for help.
- Normally, thin pink or straw-colored fluids are copiously pro-

duced immediately prior to and throughout Stage II labor. If black, thick, odorous fluid is seen before the first puppy is born, consult immediately with your veterinarian. The same is true if a thick, yellow, foul discharge is seen during the parturition process. Green-colored fluids normally accompany parturition beginning a few minutes before the first puppy is delivered and lasting throughout the delivery process.
- If a bitch seems depressed, disoriented, vomits (or attempts to vomit), acts weak, or staggers when walking, seek professional advice immediately.

How to Recognize and Assist Dystocias

There are several situations in which you should provide delivery assistance, either by physically helping or by contacting your veterinarian. Dystocias may be relieved by assisting puppies' birth with manual manipulation, by instrumentation, or by cesarean section delivery. Instrument use and surgery should be left to a veterinarian; however you may be able to help with delivery under some circumstances.

Sometimes, a dam does not remove the thin, almost transparent placental bag from the pup's head, and the pup remains half in and half

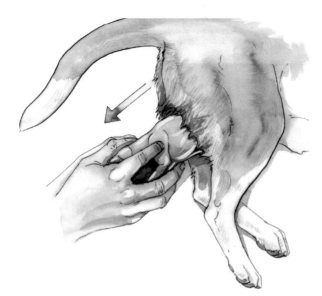

To assist birth, gentle traction is applied to shoulders of puppy.

out of the birth canal for more than three or four minutes. In that position, its life-supporting placental attachment to the uterus is seperated. In its attempt to breathe, the puppy can aspirate (inhale) placental fluid and drown, or it may succumb to a lack of oxygen. That situation occurs most commonly when a bitch has a large litter, and she simply tires late in whelping.

- With one of the clean dry towels or washcloths you have set aside, gently remove the placental membranes from the puppy's head. If the mother has ceased to apply abdominal pressure to push the pup from the canal, grasp its shoulders with the cloth and apply gentle, slow traction.

- Do not apply traction to puppies' heads alone. To deliver a puppy without damage, it is imperative that the forelegs are extended alongside its head, and traction is applied to the shoulders. When a puppy's head and neck are exposed and the forelegs are folded backward beside its body, call for help!

- If you can't obtain help quickly, insert a well-lubricated index finger into the vagina alongside the puppy's neck and ease the forelegs out, one by one. In large bitches, the procedure is easy. In toys it is often impossible.

- The direction of traction should be parallel to the hind legs of the mother, not parallel to her spine. The canine birth canal slopes downward and backward, and your traction must be applied in that direction.

- Once you have extracted the puppy from the birth canal, firmly grasp its umbilical cord with the towel and gently apply slow traction on the placental sac that remains in the uterus. Do not try to pull the placenta from the mother using the pup as a handle on its umbilical cord. To do so might eviscerate the puppy.

- When both pup and placenta are free from the birth canal, place the puppy in front of its mother and take your seat. If she begins to lick and care for it, let her manage alone. If she totally ignores it, don't waste any time in rendering further assistance.

Resuscitating the Pup

Pick it up in the cloth, and with your index finger, open its mouth, wipe it out with a twisted corner of the cloth, wipe the membranes from its body, and gently massage its chest to stimulate respiration. As soon as it begins to breathe on its own, place it under the dam's chin, leaving the placenta attached to the puppy.

Puppies are sometimes born in rapid succession. The mother actively licks and cleans each one, but she simply falls behind in her endeavors. This problem is usually encountered with large litters and an energetic mother. If a puppy is born and its head remains covered by an amniotic sac, clean it off, massage its chest for a minute, and wipe its mouth out, then, if it is breathing and squirming, return it to its dam.

Clamping the Cord

Sometimes a whelping bitch will neglect to chew and sever puppies' umbilical cords. That is characteristic of rapid deliveries of large litters as well. If there are several pups with placentas still attached, and if the mother does not object, you can help out.

Clamp two hemostat forceps about half an inch apart on the umbilical cord about an inch and a half from the puppy. Then cut the cord between the forceps. Dip the puppy end of the cord in the bottle of disinfectant and return the pup to its mother. Leave as much cord attached to the puppy as possible;

too long is better than too short. Discard the placenta and leave the forceps attached to the puppy end of the cord for ten minutes before removing them.

If the puppy's forceps bother the dam, or if no hemostat forceps are available, tie the umbilical cords tightly with dental floss, cutting the ends of the floss close to the knot. Dip the tied end in disinfectant before returning the puppy to its dam.

Cardiopulmonary Resuscitation (CPR)

When puppies remain in the birth canal too long, they may aspirate (inhale) placental fluid. Those puppies gasp for air as mucus and fluid bubbles from their noses. Their gums, lips, and the insides of their mouths are gray or bluish in color instead of the usual bright pink. Sometimes the puppies appear lifeless and no signs of respiration are

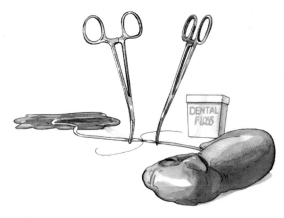

Umbilical cord should be clamped and tied, just before cutting.

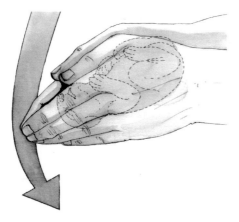

A. CPR technique showing proper placement of puppy in hands, with thumbs over chest.

evident. They are not always hopeless. Don't hesitate to try CPR, even if no heartbeats can be detected.

In such situations, you are faced with genuine emergencies and

B. Begin downward swing directly in front of you.

there is no time to call for professional help!

- Pick the puppy up with a dry cloth.
- Open its mouth by forcing the tips of your thumb and index finger between its jaws.
- Use the plastic syringe to aspirate fluids from its throat, and a twisted corner of the towel to wipe the mucus and fluid from its mouth.
- Stretch the puppy out between your two palms with its belly upward. Its head is away from you, cradled on your two index fingers. Your thumbs cover the pup's chest.
- Extend your hands and arms straight out from your body, at shoulder height, and swing your hands rapidly downward in a wide arc that ends between your knees. This swinging action applies centrifugal force and helps force fluid from the puppy's respiratory tree.
- As you swing it down, apply gentle squeezing pressure on the pup's chest with your thumbs. Relax the pressure when bringing the pup upward. The gentle chest squeezing is meant to massage the heart through its chest wall. Repeat this procedure several times.
- After three or four swings, open the pup's mouth and wipe it out with the corner of your towel, or aspirate fluid with the syringe, then repeat the procedure.

If the puppy does not respond, and does not breathe by itself, prop its mouth open with your thumb and index finger. Holding its face about two or three inches from your lips, blow into its mouth for a few seconds. Then massage its chest and swing it again. Keep repeating and don't give up on a pup in less than 30 minutes of this routine.

Posterior Births

Posterior births (hind legs first) account for four out of ten puppy deliveries. They should progress the same as anterior (head first) presentations. If you see a puppy emerging hind legs and tail first, keep close watch. If its delivery progresses at a reasonable rate, relax. A posterior presentation runs a slightly higher risk of fluid aspiration than an anterior presentation, but should be no cause for anxiety. You shouldn't wait quite as long to render assistance to a delayed posterior birth as to an anterior presentation.

If you must help a posterior birth, follow the same procedure. Grasp the puppy's pelvis and hips with a dry towel and apply gentle traction in a downward and backward direction. Quickly massage the puppy's chest for a few seconds and, if it is squirming and breathing normally, give it to its mother to clean. If the puppy is in respiratory trouble, begin CPR.

Breech Birth

Don't panic when you see only a tail emerge from the birth canal, but pay particularly close attention—breech births are always cause for concern. Most are delivered by the

C. Finish the swing between your legs.

bitch without assistance, but a few require instrumentation and sometimes cesarean section. A breech

D. If the puppy is still not breathing, blow into its open mouth from a few inches away.

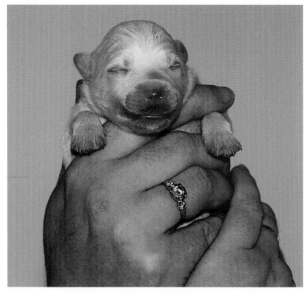
Newborn puppies should be picked up and examined shortly after birth.

sional instruction and understand the fragility of tissues that may be damaged by such manipulation. Once the hind legs are presented, the birth should progress normally.

Time is important. If you are inexperienced or unsure of the best course of action to take, call for help. Let your veterinarian either assist or walk you through the procedure on the telephone.

If your bitch is unable to deliver a breech puppy by herself, veterinary intervention will probably be necessary. Sometimes the clinician is able to deliver a breech puppy using special forceps, sometimes not. A viable option to instrumentation is a cesarean section.

When Whelping Is Finished

When the mother has finished whelping, she will usually want to go outside for a few minutes. Let her do so, but go with her! Keep her under close observation for the next 24 hours or that last, unexpected puppy might be born under a backyard tree.

After attending to her eliminations and getting a breath of fresh air, she will be anxious to return to her family. Before long, each puppy will be contentedly nursing on a full breast.

If there is any doubt whether or not all puppies have been delivered, call your veterinarian. Many clinicians prefer to palpate a bitch's

presentation is manifested by only the puppy's tail appearing in the amniotic sac. Both of its hind legs are folded forward in the birth canal, tight against its body, and only its rump and tail are visible. If the dam does not deliver the pup in five to ten minutes, call your veterinarian.

Never try to deliver a breech puppy by applying traction to its tail. If you can get a firm hold on its hips, gentle traction can be applied, but grasping the pelvis of a breech puppy is often very difficult.

In a large bitch, it is sometimes possible to insert a clean, well lubricated index finger into the birth canal alongside a breech pup and ease first one, then the other hind leg out. Do not try the technique, however, unless you have profes-

abdomen immediately following delivery, just to be sure. If doubt remains, X-ray or ultrasound imaging will add to everyone's peace of mind. Some professionals also give an injection of posterior pituitary hormone to help empty the uterus.

Note: Many professional dog breeders acquire and use injectable products themselves. I believe some owners fail to recognize the dangers involved in that practice. For example, dosage of pituitary hormone is critical and is based on several factors. Before it is injected, the reasons for its use, proper timing, its dosage schedule, and possible side effects should be considered. Dosage directions on the vial do not necessarily apply to every situation in all ages and sizes of dogs. Hormones are tricky, and incorrect use can produce reverse effects. Sometimes a single dose is indicated; other situations respond better to several smaller doses. Consult your veterinarian before you inject any product!

In giant breeds, it is often difficult to tell when whelping is finished. The fetuses are quite small compared to the deep chest and heavy abdomen of their dams, especially in breeds like Newfoundlands, Saint Bernards, and Great Pyrenees. Definitive diagnosis by abdominal palpation is very difficult or impossible, and veterinarians frequently employ X-ray or ultrasound imaging to be sure no puppies are retained.

Contented neonatal litter at the breakfast table.

Environmental Temperatures

Raising the ambient or floor temperatures of nurseries and nesting boxes can be another terrible mistake.

Example: Once, an over-cautious owner placed several sun lamps in a small bathroom that served as a maternity ward because he wanted to avoid chilling the dam and litter of fox terrier puppies. The result of his folly was a fatigued, panting, dehydrated mother and two nearly baked newborn puppies. The remaining (dead) puppy was delivered by cesarean. The bitch's temperature was 105°F (40°C), and it was necessary to stabilize her with intravenous fluids before operating.

I had other similar experiences, most of them involving heating pads placed under the whelping box. While chilling is dangerous, it is probably not as real a problem as overheating the dam and puppies, when whelping inside your home.

If you decide to use a heating pad in a whelping or nursery box, be sure to confine it to one end of the box. The puppies must be able to move away from the source of artificial heat if they seek a cooler environment (see discussion of heating pads under Temperature, page 139).

Problems are often created by overzealous or radical actions. It is very important not to offer assistance until you are sure it is needed. Once a decision to intercede is made, your assistance should be as quick and efficient as possible. Have a good idea of what you are going to do, do it, and get back into the audience. Use common sense and moderation. Do not go beyond what is necessary to get the whelping process back on schedule.

Chapter 9
Cesarean Section

In the unlikely event that your bitch can't whelp her puppies by natural means, a cesarean section may be necessary. C-sections are important dog breeding tools that save puppies' and dams' lives and give breeders a safe option when normal delivery fails.

Cesarean sections are becoming the routine means of delivering litters of certain breeds of dogs. In some cases, surgery is scheduled at the time bitches are artificially or hand-bred. The purpose of this book is not to approve, condemn, or criticize scheduled cesarean surgery, but to present general insights into the surgical procedure.

Who Is Qualified to Perform a Cesarean?

Most companion animal veterinary practitioners are trained in canine obstetric procedures, including cesarean surgery. Dog breeders usually work closely with one or two veterinary clinicians. If those practitioners who serve your general needs are comfortable doing cesarean surgery, I advise you to use them. If they do not offer after-hours services and are not available for Sunday, evening, and holiday emergencies, have them refer you to an emergency clinic staffed with qualified surgeons.

If you wish to employ the highest academically qualified surgeon, and if you live in a large metropolitan area or near a veterinary college, you may wish to contact a board certified veterinarian with advanced degrees in surgery. You might even find one who also is a theriogenologist (specialist in canine reproduction).

In either case, spend some time talking to the veterinarian. Discuss cesarean surgery experience and out-of-hours availability for emergencies, then follow your instincts. Ask other breeders in the area how they handle cesarean potentials. Cesarean sections are rarely necessary, but you should be prepared, just in case.

Risk Factors

Some risk is involved any time an animal is anesthetized. Surgery adds to that risk. Surgical procedures performed on an animal already under stress should also be considered. Another consideration is the pregnant female's anemia at term pregnancy. The massive quantity of tissue taken from a bitch in a cesarean increases shock risk. Impaired breathing ability can be a complicating factor, especially when considering the brachycephalic breeds (English bulldog facial types).

Anesthetic time and surgical time, related to the number of puppies delivered, influence both recovery time and risk. The number of previous c-sections are another factor to consider, since any abdominal surgery may stimulate adhesion formation, scars, and other potential complications for future operations.

Many veterinary surgeons advise breeders to limit the number of cesarean sections performed on an individual bitch. If you have been so advised, plan accordingly. Only the person performing an operation has an intimate knowledge of organ and tissue condition that may affect the safety of future operations. That person also has the best possible information on how a patient responded to the anesthetic used.

Those risks mentioned are inherent in every cesarean operation, but there are many ways to minimize risks as well. The pertinent risk factors can only be evaluated and calculated by examination at the time of surgery. Appropriate actions taken at that time will reduce the risks, both to the dam and her puppies.

It is the opinion of many, including the author, that a bitch's general disposition or temperament influences surgical risk. I also believe the way an animal is handled immediately prior to surgery is important. One that is excited, surrounded by chaos, worried owners, and a frenzied car ride to the animal hospital increases surgical risk. Keep cool, and provide a quiet, tranquil environment. Offer love and support to your dog through gentle petting, soft voices, and calm assurance.

Anesthesia

In recent years, we have truly come a long way concerning c-section anesthetic choices. With the advent of new injectable products and inhalation gasses, anesthesia is not as dangerous to dams and puppies as it formerly was. Anesthetic products now available do not pass the placental barrier to a significant extent, which means a bitch can be anesthetized without sedating the puppies at the same time. Puppies delivered by cesarean are not as depressed today as with older types of anesthetics. Their vital signs are usually excellent, and they nurse sooner and more aggressively.

Contemporary anesthetics allow rapid recovery of a bitch. She is ready to clean and nurse her brood very soon after the surgery is completed. There are fewer cases of litter rejection, and fewer problems with milk production. She is up and about quickly and is often eating within hours after surgery.

There is no single agent that is best under all circumstances. The scope of this book does not allow a discussion of specific anesthetic techniques, since there are many, and their efficacy is related to the surgeon performing the operation.

Spinal or epidural anesthesia may work well in one practitioner's hands, while another has more positive experience and is more comfortable using another technique. The number of puppies, size of the bitch, degree of fatigue, dehydration, or anemia all influence the type of anesthetic used. A bitch that has been in exhaustive labor for several hours requires less sedation than one who is strong and alert.

I recommend that you discuss with your veterinarian the type of anesthesia he or she intends to use. Breeders need to understand what to expect from the dam, possible anesthetic side effects, danger signs, and a definition of normal recovery.

It is vital that you furnish your veterinary surgeon with a complete history of the dam's past surgical experiences. Some anesthetic agents have an adverse side effect on various internal organs of a patient. Perhaps they should be alternated with other products if repeated c-sections are expected. Disclosure of past drug sensitivities is important as well.

When to Perform a Cesarean

Proper timing of surgery is critical. Excluding scheduled c-sec-tions, most cesareans address emergencies and are done only in the event of dystocia that can't be managed by more conservative means (see Chapter 8, Dystocia, beginning on page 87). Abdominal surgery is never the first choice for delivering a litter; however, it is a life-saving option.

It is safer for both dam and litter to perform the operation before a bitch is fatigued from long, unproductive labor. A tired, weak patient is a poor surgical candidate. If nonproductive Stage II labor is continued for more than an hour, contact your veterinarian. Risk is increased by waiting too long and minimized by prompt action. Sometimes a simple, quick blood test or two indicates the need for medication, intravenous fluid therapy, or other support techniques prior to or at the time of surgery.

The decision to perform surgery can't be made without a thorough examination of the bitch. Sometimes manual manipulation will avert the need for surgery. In cases of minor uterine fatigue, an injection of pituitary hormone will occasionally restart active labor.

Timing of required surgery, as you can see, is subject to evaluation of each dam's status. Once a definite need for surgery is established, it should be done as soon as practical.

Surgical Technique

This discussion is intended to acquaint the breeder with the general, visible stages of cesarean section surgery. There are many technical points and procedures that are omitted purposefully. It is not our intent to teach readers to perform surgery, but to inform them about what is happening.

- After the patient is shaved, prepped, anesthetized, and draped, the operation begins. The surgeon may use a flank or ventral midline incision. (A flank incision runs more or less parallel to the last rib, extending from above the mammary glands toward the spine. A ventral midline is make along the center of the abdomen, extending several inches behind the navel, midway between the mammary glands.) Each approach has its advantages and disadvantages, and the surgeon's choice is based on many factors. A rather long incision is made through the abdominal wall, clamps are placed on small bleeding vessels, and the gravid uterus is gently lifted out and supported on drapes covering the dog's abdomen.
- An incision is made in the body of the uterus. No puppies are usually attached in that portion of the uterus, but the single incision allows fetuses to be manipulated from both horns to the surgical opening.
- Puppies are individually moved to the uterine body incision and one by one they are lifted out, together with their placental membranes.
- The surgeon typically removes the amniotic sac from each puppy's face with a sterile sponge, then hands the puppy to an assistant. There is a copious amount of fluid and small amount of blood accompanying this surgery. For safety sake, the surgery must progress rapidly.
- As soon as all puppies are delivered, the uterine incision is sutured in a special way to minimize scar and adhesions. The body wall incision is then closed, and the bitch is again examined.

Assisting with a Cesarean

There are no standards governing who assists a surgeon in c-sections. They are emergency procedures, often done with little notice and out of usual business hours. Solo cesarean operations are certainly possible, but they increase the time and risk of the operation and every veterinarian I know wants help. In our practice, we preferred another veterinarian as an assistant. If a partner was unavailable, we used one of our trained technicians who knew sterile technique procedures and had experience with the operation.

Our animal hospital was many mountainous miles away from the nearest veterinarian, and nearly 200 miles from an emergency clinic. Occasionally, neither my partner nor our hospital technicians were available. In those instances, middle-of-the-night cesareans made use of my sons' or my wife's help.

They observed many operations, were carefully trained, and became quite proficient assistants.

In today's urban world, 24-hour emergency clinics are staffed with trained technicians ready to assist. General practitioners may have assistants on call and many large clinics have interns available.

Some breeders want to help. If you are among them, be sure to discuss that possibility with your veterinarian in advance of the need. If the surgeon consents, you will probably be walked through the procedure before parturition time is near. You may be advised to observe a trained assistant in action before you are allowed to participate. I watched a couple of owners break out in a cold sweat and attain a rather pale blue facial color when watching a typical, uncomplicated cesarean.

If you find your bitch in need of cesarean surgery outside of regular hours, in the absence of trained help, your veterinarian may ask you to assist. Professional dog breeders make excellent assistants. They know all about handling newborn puppies, and have wiped, rubbed, and revived puppies from natural births. About all they need to be told is to keep their hands out of the surgical field and stand well back until a puppy is dropped into their receiving towels. Usually they are kept so busy they don't have time to think about the procedure and therefore don't respond adversely to the surgery.

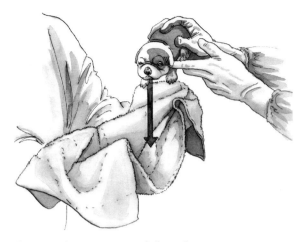

Surgeon drops cesarean-delivered puppy into receiving towel held by assistant.

In the event you assist, there are a few specific general instructions to note.

- When helping a speedy surgeon, it is important to listen carefully to all instructions given beforehand, and work quickly after the operation begins.
- After her abdomen is shaved, anesthesia is induced, and the bitch is on the surgery table, only a few minutes are required to prep her skin. Following that, a few more minutes are used scrubbing, gloving, draping, and less than a minute is required to make the abdominal incision. Another 20 seconds is required to lift the gravid uterus out of the abdomen, and a puppy is handed to you a few seconds later. Often, only 30 seconds will elapse between deliveries.
- The veterinarian will furnish the assistant a surgical gown, mask,

The contentment illustrated by this husky dam is typical of a well-conditioned mother with healthy puppies.

cap, and gloves. Except in peculiar situations, the cesarean assistant's job is to stand at the foot of the surgery table, keeping body, face, and hands well back from the patient. The veterinarian will advise you where to stand and how to receive puppies as they are taken from the uterus. I preferred to have the assistant hold a sterile surgical towel in a slinglike fashion and let me drop the puppy and its placenta into the sling.

- As soon as a puppy is received, the assistant must work quickly to remove the remaining placental membranes from its body, briskly rub its chest, wipe mucus from its nostrils and mouth, and place it in an incubator or receiving box. Between deliveries you must check on the puppies' respiration, watch for bubbles from their noses, and aspirate fluids from their throats and mouths with a syringe. It is a very busy

time, especially when more than one or two puppies are delivered.
- When all are delivered, the surgeon is occupied for a much longer time, suturing the several layers of uterus, another few layers of abdominal muscle (in flank approaches), and finally, the skin. During that time, the assistant can more completely dry the pups, perform CPR on any that seem weak (see page 93 for procedure), and clamp umbilical cords with hemostats that have been furnished for that purpose.

Often, an oxygen tank fitted with a tiny flexible plastic tube is available in small animal surgeries. When a cesarean-delivered puppy has difficulty breathing, or seems weak, the tiny oxygen tube is placed loosely just inside the pup's nostril. A few minutes of pure oxygen will make an amazing difference in the vitality of weak pups.

- Drugs are sometimes injected into weak puppies through their umbilical cords. If that technique is employed, the surgeon will give specific instructions.
- About the time the last puppy is delivered, the surgeon may instruct the assistant to administer an intramuscular hormone injection into the hind leg of the bitch. It is used to stimulate milk production as well as uterine involution (return to its normal size and shape) and emptying.
- By the time the operation is finished, the dam is waking, and she is often given some pure oxygen

to brighten her. She is examined again, her temperature is taken, and sometimes another blood sample is checked in the laboratory to better assess her state of anemia.

Release from the Hospital

Providing there are no surgical complications, both mother and litter are typically sent home as soon as possible after surgery. If you drop off your bitch at a surgical facility, be ready to pick her up within an hour or two. It is important to return the bitch to familiar home surroundings as soon as practical.

Rarely are medications prescribed following uncomplicated surgery. In case of operations complicated by ruptured uterus, dead puppies, or a weak or toxic bitch, hospitalization may be necessary. Sometimes, when the bitch requires extensive post-surgical, in-patient treatment, the puppies will be sent home to be bottle-fed until the bitch has recovered. Those situations are dealt with on an individual basis and generalities serve no purpose.

Aftercare of the Bitch and Puppies

Following surgery, puppies should be separated from the bitch until she is bright and alert. The puppies may be placed with the dam under supervision to allow nursing, but don't leave them alone together until her temperature has returned to normal and she is normally responsive. If she is allowed to be with them unsupervised while still drowsy, she may unintentionally injure them.

During the period of separation, keep the puppies' environment at a constant 90°F (32°C) temperature. It is important to continually monitor the temperature of their bedding, whether in an incubator or a shoebox. Try not to allow more than one degree temperature variation in their environment.

If the c-section was not complicated, long-term aftercare of both dam and litter is not much different than in a natural whelping. The primary difference is the surgical incision. It is not bandaged, and usually is ignored by both bitch and puppies. In some cases, especially when a midline incision is made, the crease between her full mammary glands promotes moisture collection on the suture line and surface bacteria may cause itching. If you notice the dam licking or chewing her sutures, contact the surgeon immediately.

Postsurgical Complications

Usually there are no complications from a routine cesarean section performed on a healthy bitch. It is not our purpose to use fear tactics, but potential postsurgical

A Yorkshire terrier dam and her scruffy pups. It takes more than a year to grow the long silky coat.

protrude from the abdominal incision. Report it immediately. When that wicklike fatty tissue is subjected to bacterial contamination from bedding, the bitch's tongue, or puppies, an infection may result. Peritonitis, or a generalized intraabdominal infection can be life-threatening; it is difficult to treat, but easy to prevent. Check the skin incision frequently each day for at least one week, until sutures are removed, or until the wound is sealed and dry.

Evisceration is an extremely rare but possible complication. When it occurs, it is usually associated with a bitch that has a propensity to be a worrier. If your c-section patient likes to pick and chew at her toes or licks her skin raw due to a little hair mat, give frequent attention to her surgical wound.

Evisceration occurs when a suture line fails, usually caused by trauma from a patient's persistent chewing. As sutures are removed, a string of omentum emerges. If that goes unnoticed and the trauma persists, the opening enlarges and loops of small intestine may follow the omentum. Evisceration, or the complications related to it, may be fatal. At best, surgery and intensive therapy are required to treat the problem.

complications should be discussed. To avert them, watch the surgical patient carefully. Worst case scenarios may illustrate the importance of contacting the veterinarian immediately.

If a bitch begins removing sutures, a tiny piece of fatty tissue called *omentum* (a broad, flat membrane with fatty deposits that hangs loosely in the abdominal cavity) may

Chapter 10

Lactation

Lactation refers to the period of milk production and puppy nursing. It begins at the time of whelping and ends when the puppies are weaned and the dam's milk production ceases. A bitch's health is under considerable stress during those six or seven weeks, regardless of litter size. The degree of stress is relative to litter size, diet, bitch's temperament, puppies' growth pattern, and care and condition of the dam prior to and during pregnancy.

Appetite Paradox

Typically, brood bitches' appetites are reduced for a few days during estrus, reaching their lowest about the time of ovulation. Appetites return to normal levels following mating, remain there for a week or so, then gradually increase during pregnancy. Their appetites usually wane again for a few days about 20 days after breeding. For about a week prior to parturition, their appetites diminish considerably, and if labor is prolonged or complicated, food consumption may not return to normal until several days after whelping.

This erratic appetite curve doesn't parallel nutritional requirements. Energy expenditures are high during the activity and stress of breeding. At 20 days gestation, embryos are in an active growth phase and we would expect high energy demands. Maturing fetuses during the last week of pregnancy also place high nutritional demands on the dam. The enormous energy expended during whelping needs compensatory energy intake.

I can't explain the appetite paradox, but I use it to stress the importance of careful attention to lactation nutrition (see below). Appetite and nutritional demand fluctuations during estrus and gestation graphically point out the need for dietary stability during lactation.

Lactation Nutrition

We have previously discussed the significance of complete and balanced diets prior to and during breeding and pregnancy (see Chapters 2, 3, and 6). Lactation nutrition is equally or more important.

Radical changes in diet during lactation are dangerous and should be avoided. Instead, sound nutrition should be established before breeding and continued through pregnancy and lactation. If premium, energy-dense foods are fed year round, the only changes necessary are increases or decreases in quantities fed, and perhaps supplementation at certain times of the reproductive cycle.

Premium quality dog foods labeled *complete and balanced diet*, *suitable for pregnant and lactating bitches* are available (see pages 22–28). Foods carrying the AAFCO label statement contain optimum nutrition for all phases of canine reproduction. They are researched and formulated by animal feeding tests in addition to ingredient analysis. Information relative to feeding trials is available from manufacturers.

Within a day or two following normal parturition, a dam's nutritional requirements increase dramatically. Not only does she need to compensate for decreased caloric intake during the last week of pregnancy, she must now produce milk for her offspring. The increased energy requirements are sometimes complicated by a good mother's reluctance to leave her puppies.

If she does not regularly leave her litter to eat, encourage her to do so by mixing her food with water. Make it more tasty by adding a bit of bland, low-fat beef or chicken broth, but don't suddenly begin supplementation with meats or rich foods. Digestive upsets and diarrhea brought on by unaccustomed

foods will further drain her energy and increase the energy deficit she already faces.

Table food treats, especially highly seasoned scraps of human foods, may have an adverse effect on puppies as well. Whatever you feed the nursing dam is expected to appear in her milk and enter the puppies' systems. Would you feed chili to a week-old puppy? Don't feed it to its mother.

A lactating bitch's nutritional requirements usually peak about three to four weeks after whelping. At that peak, her caloric energy needs are expected to be triple (sometimes quadruple) her prebreeding maintenance requirements. At about that time, if the puppies begin eating solid food, their demand on the dam decreases, she begins to lose interest in nursing them, and her caloric needs begin to diminish. That is not to suggest that you should wean the puppies at three or four weeks of age (see Solid Food Introduction, pages 144–145, and Chapter 13, Weaning, beginning on page 146).

Normal Variations

So far, our discussion of lactation nutrition presupposes that all dogs are alike. We know better, but the information can be used in a general way. It applies to normal circumstances, average bitches with average-sized litters and average temperaments (if such a situation exists).

Example: I raised and bred an AKC Champion Alaskan malamute bitch that didn't read this book. She exhibited very obscure signs of proestrus, and her standing heat lasted only one day. She was successfully kennel bred; that is, she was housed with a proven stud during proestrus and estrus. She was allowed free choice premium dry food from proestrus until weaning. Her dietary intake began a slow, smooth, upward curve from mating time, peaking at twice her maintenance level a month after whelping. There were no measurable fluctuations in her appetite curve during estrus, diestrus, or lactation. She exercised vigorously throughout pregnancy and lactation, and would have joined a sled team if allowed. Whelping time was difficult to predict, and was only estimated by recording her temperature three times a day during the last week of gestation.

Her three and five puppy litters grew very rapidly. When three or four weeks old, they began eating her dry food, at which time she refused to allow them to nurse any longer. The litter was fed three times a day and a creep feeder gave them constant access to dry food. To prevent obesity, the bitch's free choice feeding was stopped when she stopped feeding her puppies, and her diet was reduced to the maintenance level. She continued to clean, sort, and play with the pups until they were physically removed from her several weeks later. She maintained a beautiful coat year round, with no excessive shedding,

and her milk production ceased without discomfort or dietary reduction. Her normal weaning technique was certainly *not* average.

Small litters. Another normal, nutritional variation relates to bitches with very small litters. Pomeranians and other toys often produce litters of one or two puppies. Their maintenance energy demands are extremely low, and sometimes it is impossible to measure the increases or decreases during pregnancy and lactation. Owners of free-fed toy breeds have commented they see no appreciable change of food consumption throughout the reproductive cycle.

Large and giant breed puppies. They grow at tremendous rates and their nutritional growth requirements, combined with large litter numbers, may create a demand so great it can't be met by their dam. She may be free-fed high density foods, but is unable to consume sufficient quantities to maintain desirable weight and condition. Sometimes it is necessary to supplement those puppies' diets from birth to reduce stress in the dam (see discussion on neonatal nutrition in Chapter 12). Without bottle feeding a commercial formula, puppy growth could be retarded, puppies might be lost, and nutritional stress on the dam could be unmanageable.

The reader is referred to the nutritional discussion in Chapter 3 for information on quality and types of dog foods. Free-feeding of a premium food prevents many problems

in lactating animals, and is recommended when possible, but it is impractical with some dogs for various reasons, including obesity.

Exercise

Many bitches must be encouraged to leave their litters, especially in the first two weeks. Some refuse to leave the whelping box except when taken out on a leash. For the first few days following whelping, your bitch should be left with her puppies as much as she wishes. After that time, take her for a walk several times a day, even if only for a few minutes. Fresh air and exercise are very important for her general health and optimum milk production.

As soon as possible, stimulate play periods with her. Interest her in a chew toy or play ball with her. She won't be ready for rough-and-tumble games with children for a few weeks, but frequent periods of exercise are important. During the times she is away from her brood, be sure no one disturbs them. That is especially important for the first few days, and particularly with a bitch's first litter. If a nursing dam suspects strangers are disturbing her puppies, she may neglect her own health and refuse outdoor exercise to protect the litter. Handling the puppies is fine, but do so in her presence, allowing her to participate in your examinations of the newborns.

Caring for a New Mother

Routine handling, grooming, and usual training procedures should be reinstated within a week after whelping. Less time can be spent in those activities at less frequent intervals, but they are as important as before she was bred. For the first few days, work with her in the room where her litter is located. Let her know that your relationship with her hasn't changed. Soon her bonding trust is reinforced and she will begin to relax and respond when you call her from the whelping box.

Grooming

Grooming is now more important than usual. Normally, even when on the best possible diet, a lactating bitch loses coat. Shedding is often copious, and combing and brushing will help remove the dead coat and make her more comfortable.

Another note of caution is in order: When a lactating bitch loses patches of coat, owners often over-respond. Adding vitamin-fatty acid coat supplements to a nursing female's diet may cause diarrhea, adding to the nutritional stress that caused the shedding.

Bathing

A significant vaginal discharge of sticky, stringy, greenish fluid persists for at least two or three weeks. It tends to soil bedding, tails, and hind legs, even if the hair was clipped short. As the discharge begins to diminish, bathing will remove dead coat, clean her body, and do away with a sometimes unpleasant odor; however, bathing a lactating dam should be delayed for a reasonable period of time after whelping.

Pay particular attention to the kind of soap used to bathe your lactating bitch. Remember that her puppies nurse a dozen times a day. They cuddle under her legs and neck, crawling under her flanks and over her back. It isn't uncommon to find an aggressive pup trying to nurse its mother's ear or tail. Don't expose the newborn to chemicals or insecticides that may be detrimental to their health. Use only a bland shampoo, one that is free from all flea or tick killers, deodorants, oils and de-tanglers. Some canine shampoos are acceptable; many are not. If in doubt, use a human baby shampoo.

Rinse her coat thoroughly with plenty of warm water. Don't use cream rinses or other treatments in the rinse water. Dry her with towels and, if necessary, with a warm-air hair dryer. Don't send her back to the litter with a dripping wet coat.

Caring for Mammary Abrasions

Owners sometimes notice scratches on and around mammary nipples. Redness, small abrasions, and toenail marks are common. If those lesions are tender to your

A proud Newfoundland dam and her brood pose for the camera on the dining room floor.

touch or if you notice the dam wincing when a puppy begins to nurse and knead with its forefeet, you may be inspired to medicate them to give her some comfort. Maybe you shouldn't!

If you apply medicine to mammary lesions, be very careful what you use. Bag Balm, cortisone creams, vitamin A and D ointments, and other products are sometimes applied and rubbed in but they are quickly licked off and ingested by puppies, sometimes causing serious digestive problems. Even natural products like aloe vera and lanolin can upset the stomachs of neonatal pups. Human diaper rash medications are popular among novice breeders for mammary lesions but remember that human babies' bottoms are covered, and

the products used are not likely to enter the babies' digestive systems. Anything you apply to the dam will surely find its way into the puppies.

In my experience, only serious mammary abrasions should be treated. Never apply medications directly on or immediately around nipples. Lesions that are located several inches from nipples may possibly be treated with certain vanishing cream medications. Call your veterinarian or pharmacist for the names of safe products to use, and use them strictly according to directions.

Oral and injectable medications should also be carefully evaluated.

Example: I was once asked to treat a week-old litter of Irish Setter puppies for lethargy. They were nursing only sporadically, and several were losing weight. The dam's mammary glands were distended, with milk virtually dripping from her nipples. The puppies began to nurse when a nipple was directed into their mouths, but within a few seconds they fell asleep. Their respiration and heartbeats were depressed. Scattered over the floor of the whelping box, they showed little activity, only moving sluggishly with great effort.

After examining the bitch and noticing some inflammation under her forelegs, I asked if she was receiving any medication. The owners were unwittingly giving her three huge daily doses of a human antihistamine product to treat her "grass allergy." When the drug was discontinued, the puppies returned to normal activity and eating habits. She itched and scratched at her allergy lesions, but they were controlled after weaning.

Aspirin, antibiotics, and many other oral or injectable medications will be passed into a lactating bitch's milk. I suggest you review the section on drugs during pregnancy (see pages 69–70). The same recommendations apply to lactation. Don't administer anything without checking it out first with your veterinary adviser.

The Dam's Weaning Diet

Once you decide to wean your puppies, the dam's diet must again be evaluated (see Chapter 13, Weaning). As the weaning process begins, gradually reduce her diet over a period of three weeks. Refer to your written notes on her prebreeding maintenance dietary intake, as well as the increases made during gestation and lactation. As the puppies begin eating solid food, cut back the dam's food accordingly. When puppies are physically removed and no longer allowed to nurse, it is advisable to further reduce her food to less than her maintenance quantity. That level will reduce milk production and relieve the intense mammary swelling and congestion that normally follows weaning.

In other words, if her peak intake was three times her maintenance level, reduce her peak quantity by 25 percent every four days. With the first reduction, she will receive 75 percent of the peak intake, which is still more than twice her maintenance level. The second 25 percent reduction will give her slightly over half the peak level; the third reduction will be slightly over a third the peak quantity; the fourth reduction will nearly reach her maintenance level; and the fifth reduction will bring her diet slightly below her dietary maintenance level.

If she is fed three times daily, reduce each meal by one-quarter every four days. If free-fed, measure the total food consumed at her peak demand, and reduce the quantity offered by one-quarter every four days. It is important to carefully note her maintenance food

Weighing puppies is a sound management practice.

intake level and use it as your target. Remember, some bitches do not triple their energy intake during lactation.

Maintain her diet at a level slightly below maintenance until her milk production ceases, then return to her normal maintenance level.

Monitoring the Puppies

When making the dam's diet reductions, watch and weigh the puppies regularly. If they continue to gain weight and aggressively consume increasing quantities of solid food, continue the weaning process. If they lose weight or energy, make no further reduction in the dam's diet until the puppies return to normal gaining.

There are exceptions to every rule. The most notable one to the above discussion relates to a bitch with an inherently poor appetite, one that shows no appreciable increase in food consumption during pregnancy and lactation. Obviously those bitches must be evaluated individually and weaning techniques adjusted according to their needs.

A bitch that suffered increased stress during pregnancy, whelping, or lactation may reach weaning time well under the preferred body weight. Obviously it could be dangerous to her health to follow a routine dietary reduction. In such cases, professional health evaluation should dictate weaning procedures.

Another exception is the bitch with a fine appetite that self-weans her puppies. If she suddenly no longer nurses them, reduction in her diet must proceed at a more rapid pace to prevent over-feeding and obesity.

A final point must be reiterated. Changes in quality of food and supplements influence animals' diets whenever they occur. Our discussion about reproductive nutrition assumes that the breeder feeds a complete balanced, premium quality food throughout the reproductive cycle, one that is labeled and field trial-approved for use for growth, gestation, and lactation.

Chapter 11
Post-whelping Problems of the Bitch

Most postparturient problems are manifested during the first few hours after whelping. Signs of trouble may be missed due to temporary changes associated with whelping.

Hemorrhage

Although whelping is messy business, most of the early, light-colored, serous fluids are obviously not whole blood. Those watery fluid losses are often copious, especially if the litter is large and born rapidly. Later, fluids are greenish-black, or straw-colored, and some appear slightly blood-tinged. Minor bleeding from stretch wounds in the vulva might be noted, but they do not produce a significant flow of blood. It is rare to see major hemorrhage at the time of parturition.

If bleeding accompanies or follows whelping, call your veterinarian immediately. Uterine hemorrhage is a serious emergency. It can be treated with injectable products or surgical procedures, often combined with whole blood transfusion.

Prolapse

Uterine prolapse is also very rare in canines. It relates to a portion of the uterus turning inside out and protruding through the birth canal. When it occurs, it closely follows whelping and is manifested by a mass of pink tissue extending from the vulva. It causes extreme discomfort, licking at the tissue, and restlessness. It may be accompanied by hemorrhage, and an affected bitch is likely to exhibit signs of shock. Prolapse is an emergency and demands immediate attention. Even if the state of shock is minimal, it predisposes the uterus to infection and is a challenge to repair.

Treatment often requires surgical replacement, and sometimes ovariohysterectomy must be performed to prevent recurrence of the condition.

Vomiting and Diarrhea

Some postparturient problems that are perceived by owners are

A beautiful Alaskan malamute, waiting for the snow.

than she has for several days, and she may eat more food than she can digest. Overindulgence of food following whelping can also cause vomiting, but it is not accompanied by loss of appetite, weakness, or fever. Gluttony is usually seen in large breeds with big appetites.

Similar preventable vomiting and soft stools or diarrhea episodes are seen when well-meaning owners offer special treats to the post-whelping bitch. Rich or unaccustomed foods can cause a single episode of vomiting without other signs of illness.

Persistent vomiting, especially if the animal is weak, depressed, or uncoordinated, is cause for alarm. Take her temperature, and if elevated above 102°F (39°C), call your veterinarian immediately. A feverish, disoriented postparturient bitch displaying repeated vomiting needs immediate professional attention.

A black, tarry, mucoid stool is usually observed the first week after whelping. Like placenta vomiting, it is the result of a bitch's propensity to eat placental tissues. It is not a sign of disease if it gradually disappears after a few days and the stool appears normal within a week. A nursing bitch often has softer stools while she is actively consuming her puppies' excretions as well.

Mastitis

Place your palm against each mammary gland. If one or more are hot and tender to your touch, gently

not really problems at all. For instance, many dams vomit food for their young. That event usually occurs when the puppies are four to six weeks old, and is an effective, if messy, natural canine system for starting pups on solid food.

Vomiting immediately following whelping can be expected in some cases as well. Bitches normally consume some, if not all, placentas as they appear. Sometimes eating even one will stimulate emesis a few hours later. Any time vomiting occurs, the material regurgitated should be inspected and identified. It's a nasty job, but important in determining the cause of vomiting.

After her puppies are safely delivered, a bitch may feel better

grip and squeeze the base of the nipple. If bloody or thick yellow fluid is produced, suspect mastitis (infection of the milk-producing tissue). Take her temperature, evaluate her appetite, and contact your veterinarian.

Remember that normal colostrum is slightly thicker and darker than normal milk. When you suspect mastitis, milk a few drops from each of several glands, including the one that feels hot and tender. The differences between colostral milk and mastitis exudate should be very apparent.

Mastitis may affect a single gland or all productive glands. It is a serious disease and warrants immediate medical attention. Bitches can become toxic from absorption of poisons produced by bacteria within the infected gland(s). If vomiting accompanies mastitis, it is usually associated with toxemia. In those cases, the bitch usually loses her milk supply, at least temporarily, and often requires intensive care, including intravenous therapy.

Mastitis, if not corrected early, can also result in abscess formation within a mammary gland. That condition is also very dangerous, and usually requires surgical intervention.

Retained Placenta and Pups

Persistent vomiting accompanied by dehydration, lack of appetite, depression, and weakness may result from a retained placenta or, more commonly, a retained puppy. Usually those conditions are accompanied by some degree of uterine infection (metritis) and temperature elevation.

Signs of retained placentas or puppies may follow parturition immediately, or several days later. Diagnosis can be made by abdominal palpation, X-rays, or ultrasound imaging. Treatment depends on the individual situation. Hormone injections, vaginal infusions, and intravenous fluid therapy can be employed. Surgical procedures may be considered, and systemic antibiotics are usually necessary.

As with all systemic diseases, there is great danger in procrastination. Get professional help at once.

Eclampsia

Eclampsia is often called canine milk fever, and is referred to in technical literature as *puerperal tetany*. I've seen the condition during late pregnancy and during the first three weeks of lactation. Reports in literature refer to eclampsia occurrences as late as weaning time, but I believe it to be rare at that stage of lactation.

Its association with calcium metabolism has long been recognized, but the exact mechanism triggering it is still debated. Early investigators found an association between eclampsia and the parathyroid gland that is responsible for maintaining blood levels of calcium.

*Boxers
courting.*

The condition occurs more frequently in small breeds of dogs, notably in toys, but I have treated it in dogs as large as setters, and once in an Irish Wolfhound. In many cases, it seems to be associated with litter size compared to the size of the bitch. A five-pound bitch with three or four pups is probably at greater risk than a 20-pounder with the same number of offspring. Probably all breeds are susceptible under the right circumstances.

Personal observation hints at the possibility of inherited factors involved with eclampsia. I can offer no proof, but have seen eclampsia prevalent in certain bloodlines of two or three small breeds. Those bitches were closely line-bred and produced relatively large litters,

which may be the reason for the perceived eclampsia predisposition.

Signs

The signs of eclampsia are dynamic and not easily missed. It usually occurs during the first few days of lactation. At first, bitches are nervous, restless, pacing, panting, salivating, and in obvious distress. They pay little attention to their maternal duties, often seeking the comfort of their owners. Within a few minutes to an hour they walk with difficulty, often staggering and falling. They progress next to convulsive paddling of all legs while lying on their side with neck and head arched backward. Those signs may take minutes or hours to develop. Eventually, if no therapy is initiated, the bitch becomes toxic, her mucous membranes become dark and congested, her heart rate increases, and the condition can be fatal.

Eclampsia is an emergency. The progressive condition can be reversed at any stage if treated. Don't wait until a convenient time to call your veterinarian—this is definitely not a condition that invites home therapy!

Treatment

Treatment response is as dynamic as the disease symptoms. Placing a needle and catheter into veins of tiny, convulsing bitches is a challenge for a veterinary clinician, but it must be done. Once an intravenous catheter is in place, slow administration of a calcium solution is maintained until response is seen. Within a very short time, the convulsing, prostrate bitch is standing, wagging her tail, bright and alert as ever! It takes but a few minutes to reverse the symptoms unless the condition reaches an advanced stage. Comatose animals may or may not respond well to treatment. When convulsions last more than a few minutes, bitches are quite fatigued and often sleep for hours after treatment.

Response to intravenous calcium is monitored by your veterinarian with a stethoscope as calcium metabolism is intimately involved with cardiac muscle activity. Strength and rate of heart contractions must be followed closely as the medication is given. Too much injected calcium can be as bad as too little.

Aftercare

Aftercare consists of intramuscular or subcutaneous calcium injections, oral calcium supplementation, and careful observation by the owners for repeated attacks. Puppies are separated from the dam for a day or two, and are bottle-fed a replacement formula during that time. Repeated attacks of eclampsia often necessitate orphan-raising the litter.

Prevention

In an effort to prevent eclampsia, some breeders feed calcium supplements during the last half of pregnancy and throughout lactation. I can't defend or deny the value of that program; it seems to be effective in a few cases, and fail in others. If carefully implemented, the practice should be harmless. I caution all breeders to use discretion when choosing the dosage and type of supplement used, and discuss possible side effects with their veterinarian before beginning calcium supplementation.

Metritis

Metritis refers specifically to uterine inflammation, but the inflammation is usually associated with infection. Uterine infections are emergencies that can be fatal if not treated quickly and effectively.

Signs

In postparturient bitches, metritis often follows dystocias and prolonged labor. Purulent, foul discharge exudes from the uterus through the still dilated cervix and vagina. All the usual signs of an acute or severe systemic infection accompany metritis—fever, weakness, depression, dehydration, dull eyes, listlessness, and reduced milk production.

Veterinary examination often reveals an enlarged, soft uterus that is painful when palpated. Blood counts confirm acute bacterial infection, and therapy begins immediately.

Therapy

X-rays or ultrasound imaging may be used to search for causes of the infection, such as retained puppies or placental tissue. Other causes may be associated with poor whelping hygiene, especially when human assistance was involved. Dirty bedding and general kennel sanitary conditions are sometimes incriminated. Whatever the cause, the condition requires vigorous therapeutic measures to save the bitch's life.

In many cases of metritis, surgical treatment is the safest option. Ovariohysterectomy presents some surgical risk, but often it represents a more positive approach and less risk than conservative therapy. Surgery is supported by antibiotic and fluid therapy.

With acute metritis, the puppies must be separated from their dam and bottle fed, at least until the condition is resolved and the dam's milk is free from toxins and drug residues. A bitch that is spayed to cure metritis may regain milk production when her body is relieved from the stress of infection and surgery, but don't count on it too heavily.

In less acute cases or when the animal's reproductive future takes precedence in the decision-making process, intravaginal infusions of antibiotics and other antibacterial agents are used. Unfortunately, it is nearly impossible to safely infuse antibacterial products directly into the uterus. Intravenous antibiotics, prostaglandin, and fluid therapy are other important tools used in nonsurgical therapy.

Effect on Puppies

Systemic, infectious conditions have their primary effects on the bitches; some may threaten their lives. In addition, bacterial toxins absorbed into their bloodstreams wind up in their milk and may be hazardous to nursing puppies. Antibiotics used against systemic infections may also be passed to the puppies and have serious detrimental effects on them.

Any time a nursing bitch becomes ill, consider how best to protect the puppies as you treat their dam. Sometimes raising them as orphans is the best course of action (see Rearing Orphan Puppies, pages 137–142). Confer with your veterinarian about the situation.

Hyperplastic Nipples

Usually a condition of older bitches, nipples become overgrown with callous-like tissue. The condition usually results from age and repeated trauma of puppies' teeth and toenails. There is no great significance to the condition unless the puppies' mouths are too small to fit over the enlarged nipples. Fortunately, hyperplasia often doesn't affect all of a bitch's nipples, and it rarely demands bottle-feeding the puppies.

An American Eskimo dam relaxes with her newborn brood.

Milk Duct Atresia

If puppies routinely avoid nursing from a particular mammary gland, try squeezing a drop or two of milk from the nipple with your thumb and index finger. If you are unable to do so, it may be due to lack of normal openings of the milk ducts.

Having as many as a dozen glands, a bitch usually has sufficient sources of milk for a good-sized litter even with one gland out of production. If the pups are all doing well and the obstructed gland is not painful and hot, it can be ignored. That gland's milk production will cease very soon, and it will shrink back to normal size.

Veterinarians are sometimes successful in opening the nipple ducts. Consult with your veterinary clinician before you schedule an appointment.

Chapter 12

Neonatal Puppy Care

The term "neonatal" refers to newborn animals, usually those during their first month of life. We will extend the term to include puppies from birth to weaning age or about six or seven weeks old. Canine neonates mature rapidly and quickly become independent individuals. During those first weeks of life, they have certain needs peculiar to the species.

Moving the Puppies

If a dam is uncomfortable with the nursery provided, she may elect to move her litter. That is another important reason for establishing a whelping place and nursery in a restricted, confined area such as a spare room or bathroom. If not confined, don't be surprised if you hear puppies under your bed or behind the sofa.

When novice breeders first see a bitch carrying a puppy, they fear the worst. Often she will have the pup's head inside her mouth, its body hanging limply from her jaws. It appears you have caught her in the act of cannibalism. Don't be alarmed—just direct her back to the nursery and confine her there.

Moving the pups is a sign that the dam is not happy with their environment. Often the diagnosis and remedy are simple. Observe human activity in the nursery. Loud noises, children playing, people handling the puppies, confusion, or human traffic are likely causes for her actions. Enforce a quiet rule, spend some time petting and reassuring her, and she will adapt.

Considerations for the Dam

If your bitch has a long coat and her abdomen was not clipped short before whelping, do so as soon as possible after all puppies are born. Be careful with your scissors or clippers—it is very easy to nick or snag a nipple with scissors or comb at this time. Don't try to shave the area; razor burn or clipper burn is very difficult to medicate while puppies are nursing. It is important to physically remove all the loose hair you trim off. Puppies are rather indiscriminate in their nursing habits and may swallow bits of her coat if they are left in the whelping box.

As soon as whelping is finished, check the dam's milk supply. With your thumb and index finger, apply gentle pressure on each nipple at its point of attachment to the mammary gland. Lightly squeezing a nipple should produce drops of milk from its openings. You will find that some glands are fuller than others, and the milk should be a creamy, off-white color. It is thicker in consistency at this time because of the colostrum (see page 136) content. After a few days, the milk will appear whiter and thinner.

After all puppies are delivered, watch them from a nearby vantage point. Observe their general attitudes as the dam rolls them about, cleaning and sorting them. Notice their nursing habits, paying particular attention to individuals that differ from the rest. Watch for weak puppies, or ones that do not respond to their dam's attention.

After 15 or 20 minutes of observation from a distance, major differences between puppies should be obvious. Again, direct your attention to pups that act differently from the others, or ones that the bitch pushes aside. Those pups should be examined immediately. If all puppies seem contented, and the bitch has settled into her new matronly role, it is time to identify the pups.

Puppy Identification

Colors and Numbers

Pick up each puppy and mark it for future reference. One of the easiest ways to individually identify pups is by painting a rear toenail or

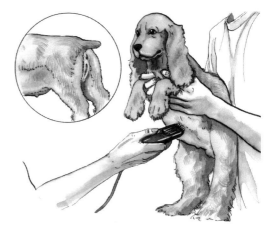

Clip long coat from abdomen and perineum prior to whelping.

two with fingernail polish. Using a different color for each pup, put a corresponding dot of the color on separate pages of a notebook, then assign numbers or letters to the various colors. You may wish to use a system of identification numbers that indicate the month and year born, the dam's initial, the sire's initial, and the sequential number of the pup.

Example: Sally's first puppy, sired by Tom, born in May, 1995 might be numbered S-5-95-T-1, the second pup of the litter is S-5-95-T-2, and so forth.

Many experienced breeders mark puppies as soon as they are born and keep records of the sequence of birth. Number 1 puppy is the first born, and so forth. In those cases, notes are made on dystocia puppies, delayed labor, those that receive CPR or any other whelping assistance.

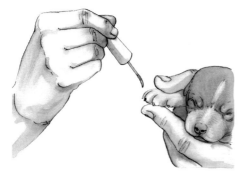
Mark puppies with nail polish of different colors.

Colored Yarn

Some references suggest identifying newborn puppies by means of colored yarn tied loosely around their necks. In practice, however, the bitch can remove the yarn, puppies can get their forefeet caught in it, and the yarn collars can even become tangled between two or three pups. I prefer fingernail polish since it rarely causes the dam any consternation, very little is used, and it only needs reapplication every four or five days. Later, consider permanently identifying the puppies.

Other Means of Identifying

There are several methods presently available for permanently marking puppies after four weeks of age.
- Placing tattoos in their flanks, on their abdomens, or undersides of ears is a time-honored system. The technique is easily learned and can be done by breeders with equipment available from pet supply stores and catalogs. The pain involved is minor and of no lasting consequence. No sedation or anesthesia is required, but cleanliness is critical since the tattoo needles penetrate into and sometimes through the tender skin. To be safe, you should have your veterinarian do this job.

Tattoos may continue to use the newborn numbering system. Visible permanent identification can be registered with national tattoo registries. For local information on those organizations, consult with your dog club officers or a veterinarian.
- Modern technology uses tiny computer chip implants that are placed beneath the skin with a hypodermic needle; however, they have the esthetic advantage of being invisible, which is also a disadvantage. On the other hand, visible tattoos may discourage theft, like visibly identified works of art or electronic equipment in your home. A visible tattoo also may help recover a lost dog that has been picked up by a well-meaning neighbor. If the dog is wearing a collar with a tag bearing your phone number, it is likely to be returned. Likewise, a visible tattoo lets the finder know that the dog belongs to someone. Establishing ownership and advertising for return of the dog becomes much easier.
- Subcutaneous microchip identification can be recorded by national registry organizations with whom the breeder is affiliated. The chips use technology

similar to that employed for pricing grocery products, and are read by scanners. Implants are done by many veterinarians as well as other trained professionals. If you wish to use that system, contact an officer of your local all-breed or specialty dog club or your veterinarian.

Puppy Records

The importance of day to day record-keeping can't be over-emphasized. A lot of information can be obtained from your experiences with each litter. Don't rely on your memory! Only accurate, detailed records can be trusted and used in the future.

Examinations and notable characteristics such as sex, weight, appetite, and personality should all be recorded from the day of whelping. In some breeds, color changes occur as puppies mature. Spots or splashes of colors change size and shape. Coat characteristics change from month to month. Some puppies are more aggressive than others. Some bond to humans quicker. You will notice those changes, but if not recorded, they will be lost by weaning time. If you are serious about breeding, complete and accurate records of the animals produced are essential. That is especially true when you select breeding stock for yourself or other purebred dog breeders.

Many conscientious dog breeders continue to follow their progeny until mature, keeping in touch with new owners, recording show wins and information on the next generation of puppies produced. The more information amassed, the better you can predict the characteristics of future litters from your dam.

Puppy Examination

When the puppies are a few hours old, as you take each one from the dam to mark with fingernail polish, look it over carefully.

- Inspect for umbilical hernias that appear as small soft, spherical enlargements under the abdominal skin at the navel. Some swelling is normal at the umbilical cord's point of attachment, but if the swelling is soft, and larger than those of other pups in the litter, make note of it. Some puppies have what appear to be small hernias, but within a week the swellings are gone and the abdomens appear normal. Other umbilical swellings continue to enlarge, and at some time in the future they require surgical correction (rarely before three to six months of age).
- Look at each leg and foot. Extra dewclaws (see page 143) are normal in some of the giant breeds, but hind and double dewclaws should be noted on your records to assure that they are removed when the pup is a few days old if required in the breed standard.
- Tail kinks are faults in most breeds, and should be noted for

Curious Irish setter pups awaiting some action.

beagles, Boston terriers, boxers, bull mastiffs, bullterriers, Chihuahuas, collies, and many other breeds. The condition is easily identified as a separation, or split, extending along the midline of the palate. Some extend the entire length of the palate; some are abbreviated, and only reach a short distance. If you suspect a cleft palate, make note of the puppy's number and watch it nurse. If milk bubbles from its nose as it swallows, or if it has difficulty nursing, swallows air, and cries a lot, your veterinarian should be contacted immediately. Even if the puppy seems to progress normally, it should receive more attention when the litter is seen by your health care professional.

future reference. In some breeds, such as the Boston terrier, a long straight tail is a fault and kinks are normal. Some breeds' standards specify that tails of a certain length are preferred. Your notes on tail conformation at birth may help you choose puppies to show or breed in the future.

- Note that the puppies' eyelids are sealed shut and their ear canals are closed as well. They will open sometime during the second week of life. Irreparable damage will be done to the eyes if you attempt to unseal the eyelids.
- Open every mouth and check for cleft palates. That recessive genetic fault plagued English bulldogs for years. It is also seen in

- While you have the pup's mouth open, look at its oral mucous membranes that cover the structures within the mouth. With a few breed exceptions (notably, the chow chow), the gums, tongue, and lips should be moist and vibrant pink. Pale gray or blue-gray membranes are signs of serious problems. They may be indications of anemia, or lack of adequate oxygenated blood in those tissues. Pale membranes are extremely important and may indicate respiratory or cardiac insufficiencies, and your veterinarian should be consulted. If in doubt as to the normal color of oral mucous membranes, compare the puppies, one to another, and to the dam.

- Check the other end of the pup. *Atresia ani* (lack of an anal opening) is a very rare condition that is sometimes treatable if discovered immediately. While in that anatomical area, determine and record the sex of each pup.
- Lay the pup in your palm and observe its respiratory rate and depth. If its breathing seems labored, rapid, and shallow, or choppy in nature, it may have an airway blockage resulting in inability to oxygenate. If you aren't sure, compare the puppy's respiratory character to that of its siblings. A pup with breathing difficulty will likely also be uncomfortable, crying, restless, and struggling. Possible causes for dyspnea (difficult breathing) are many and varied. One of the first thoughts in a newborn is fluid remaining in the trachea and upper bronchial tree. Blowing mucus bubbles from the nostrils is a sign that fluid still exists in the upper respiratory system. CPR (see pages 93–95) may eliminate that fluid and save a puppy.
- The coats of healthy newborns should be slick and shiny. With a few exceptions (shar peis and English bulldogs), skin wrinkles in newborn puppies are abnormal. When they occur, they are often signs of dehydration. Depending on the state of dehydration, puppies can be treated. Before initiating treatment, have the puppy examined by a professional. A quick, easy lab test will give the

Owner should examine puppies for deformities.

answers to type and duration of treatment needed. Very minor dehydration may correct itself in aggressively nursing puppies. Professional treatment for dehydration may involve oral fluid administration or injections of sterile electrolyte solutions.

- Lack of complete hair cover or sparse coats may indicate premature birth. Premature puppies are often weak and do not nurse well. When discovered, supplemental bottle feeding or stomach

Eyes and ears are sealed at birth.

A Bichon Frise dam and her three-week-old puppies.

colic signs. Notes should be made and bloated puppies should receive professional evaluation as soon as possible.

- Colic is a catch-all term that is applied to practically any disorder that causes puppies to exhibit signs of digestive distress. There are many remedies for colic that may or may not work, depending on the cause of the condition. I recommend that you obtain from your veterinarian a specific diagnosis of the cause of a bellyache before you administer any medication to a pup with colic. If you decide to try home remedies without benefit of specific diagnosis, be especially mindful of the intestinal absorptive rate of newborns compared to older pups. Correct dosages of all medications are calculated by the weight and age, and drugs that are safe in pups of one age and size may be fatal to younger or smaller animals.

- If a pup feels limp or flaccid when handled, and lacks vigorous behavior, it is likely in trouble. Take immediate measures to identify the problem. Weak puppies can die in less than a day if no action is taken to correct their problems.

tube (see page 138) feeding may be necessary to save them. Suspected premature pups should be examined and evaluated by your veterinarian very early to rule out congenital deformities that can complicate the picture.

- After nursing a few times, puppies' abdomens should be full but not distended. Pups with distended or bloated abdomens cry and are usually seen wandering, apart from siblings. They may try to nurse, give up, and try another nipple. Bloated pups usually demonstrate ineffective nursing, swallowing air, and exhibiting

After your examination is finished, as you replace each puppy into the nest, lay it on its back and watch its righting reflex. It should roll quickly onto its chest and begin seeking the warm safety of its dam or siblings immediately.

Weight

Record the weight of each pup. Great variations in birth weight are seen from breed to breed, but puppies generally gain between 5 and 10 percent of their birth weight per day, doubling their birth weight the first week of life. To obtain average birth weights for your particular breed, contact a breed club. Birth weights and rates of gain over the first four weeks of life are extremely important predictors of neonatal illnesses and deaths. A puppy that is born significantly below the normal average weight is a candidate for illness and merits close observation. Often those lightweight puppies lack vitality, and some are found to have circulatory problems or other congenital, internal organ anomalies.

When to weigh: Weighing the puppies daily during their first week of life is good management. Accurate scales are available at pet supply stores and catalog order houses. Dietetic scales that weigh in grams are sufficiently accurate, but grocery produce scales have a wide margin of error. Be sure to weigh the puppies about the same time each day. Although milk production is more or less constant, some dams fall into a routine and encourage nursing more heavily early mornings, and very little during the night.

Puppies are normally very strong within a few hours after birth. When handled, their bodies feel full, with firm muscle tone evident. Their skins should be very elastic, and when lifted gently over the withers,

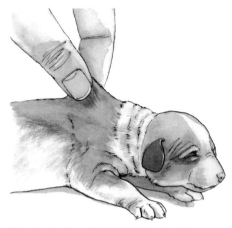

Gently pinch up fold of skin to test for dehydration. Normal skin should snap back as soon as released.

then released, skin should snap back to its normal state immediately. Healthy puppies squirm when picked up. They may cry or not, but invariably they scramble vigorously from your hand.

Temperature

Newborn puppies' body temperatures should be recorded. For the first few weeks, they mimic cold-blooded animals, with their body temperatures responding to those of their environment. Normal puppy temperature at birth is about 97°F (36°C). It should increase gradually, reaching 101.5°F (38.5°C) by the end of the third week of life.

To take their temperatures, use an oral stubby type human thermometer. Be sure the mercury is shaken down below 90°F (32°C). Lubricate it with petroleum jelly and insert it half an inch into the rectum. Keep a gentle but firm hold on both

Monitor a puppy's temperature if illness is suspected.

puppy and thermometer during the minute or two it remains in the rectum.

Thermometers. There is a new generation of human infant thermometers that is probably adaptable for use in puppies. They instantly record temperatures from within the ear canal of humans. If interested, I encourage you to try one. Be sure to check your readings with the old-fashioned rectal thermometer on a few pups to correlate the readings. And remember, puppies' ear canals don't open until they are ten days old or older.

Nesting box temperature. Nesting box ambient temperature should be kept at normal room temperature or about 75°F (24°C) unless puppies appear weak and need support. In such cases, increase the temperature at one end of the box to 85°F (29.5°C) or 90°F (36°C) for a few days.

If a single puppy is hypothermic, it can be isolated from the others for a few hours while you bring its body temperature up. By confining

it to a small space, perhaps a box just large enough for it to stretch out, it is easier to control and monitor. Keep a thermometer on the source of heat and maintain the temperature of its environment no higher than 100°F (38°C). Monitor the puppy's body temperature frequently. When its temperature reaches 97°F (36°C) and it is more active, return it to the dam.

Don't overreact to hypothermic pups! I have treated puppies that were nearly broiled with infrared heat lamps and I have heard horror stories of uninformed breeders using a kitchen oven to warm puppies. I refuse to believe an unconfirmed report of an amateur breeder using a microwave oven for the same purpose!

Sunlamps. Although sunlamps or infrared heat lamps warm the environment quickly and effectively, don't subject puppies to them; they will dehydrate the puppies quickly and are commonly incriminated in puppy deaths. Place a reliable thermometer on the puppies' bedding over the source of heat and monitor it closely. Keep it less than 90°F (32°C). Use heating pads with extreme caution, as the dam may chew wires, all pads do not generate the same amount of heat at a given setting, and they may overheat the nesting box. If using a heating pad, turn it on Low and place it under several layers of towels in such a way that puppies can freely move from it onto cooler, unheated surfaces.

Keep in mind that heating pads constantly generate heat that is dissipated into the environment. If your nursery box is covered, as with a fiberglass shipping crate, the heating pad may raise the ambient temperature within the enclosure to an intolerable temperature in a very short time. The dam may be reluctant to remain in the overheated box and your purpose is defeated.

Plastic soda bottles. Fill these with hot tap water and roll them up in towels to make good puppy warmers. Desired temperature is maintained by changing the water as it cools. Radiating their warmth in a three-dimensional fashion, they simulate the warmth of the dam, and puppies can easily snuggle up or move away from them. While replenishing hot water every few hours is a bother, it also pays off since it brings you in contact with your charges frequently and regularly. Puppies snuggling up to the warmth indicate they still need that warmth. If they all are found away from the warm bottles, you can probably discontinue that support.

Hypoglycemia

Hypoglycemia (low blood sugar) can cause puppies to exhibit weakness, difficulty breathing, and crying. Those signs are also seen with dehydration, hypothermia, and trauma. Don't overlook the possibility of a puppy being handled roughly or dropped by a child. If the cause of symptoms is in doubt, consult with your veterinarian. Lab-

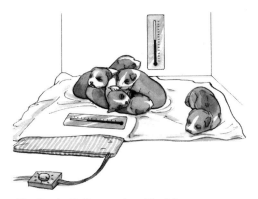

Monitor both floor and ambient temperature in orphan puppies' nursery. Always allow access to non-heated areas.

oratory tests can measure blood sugar and state of dehydration.

Treatment. Hypothermia and hypoglycemia can be treated by oral administration of certain glucose-containing electrolyte fluids. The balance of electrolytes and glucose in those fluids is very important. When 5 percent glucose alone is given orally, the usual dose is about ¼ cc per ounce of body weight. It may be repeated frequently, according to

Puppies like to snuggle against wrapped bottle of warm water.

need and response. I urge you not to give oral glucose or electrolytes without professional advice and directions. Your veterinarian will probably make recommendations over the phone, and will help you acquire the appropriate fluids.

Commercial milk replacer can be obtained from pet supply houses. Its use can also aid in correcting hypoglycemia, hypothermia, and nutritional deficits. It should be fed warm, either by bottle and nipple, or, if you are qualified, by stomach tube (see page 138). Any liquids given must be warmed to the puppy's body temperature or slightly above. If using commercial products, adhere strictly to the label's dosage instructions.

More serious cases can be treated with warmed electrolyte solutions, such as lactated Ringer's solution, administered by a veterinarian under the puppy's skin or into its vein.

Eating Habits

Normal puppies with full stomachs are usually found sleeping in a cluster when not nursing.

Make notes about the eating behavior of each pup, whether aggressive or apathetic. If a puppy is found separated from its mother, make a note on its record. If it is often separated, examine it closely; there is probably a reason. All puppies cry occasionally, and such crying is not noteworthy, but if one particular pup cries frequently and the others do not, look it over. If a reasonable diagnosis isn't made by your examination, call for help.

Crying. Restless, crying puppies are probably hungry. If one is found in that state, squeeze a drop or two of milk from a nipple, and while the milk drops are suspended on the tip, introduce the nipple into the puppy's mouth and watch closely. It may have been shoved from a breast by a stronger puppy, and when it is allowed to nurse without competition, it will fill its stomach promptly.

If most of the brood are restless and crying, moving from nipple to nipple, the bitch should be thoroughly examined. Take her temperature. Check the milk supply from each gland (see Mastitis, page 116, and Milk Duct Atresia, page 121). If her milk production is inadequate to meet puppy demand, review her diet, both quality and quantity, and have her examined. It is probably prudent to shop for bottles, nipples, and replacement formula as well.

Eyelids and Ear Canals

Record the day your puppies' eyelids separate and when their ear canals open. There is some variation in those times among different breeds. Eyelids begin to separate at about 10 days of age, and ear canals open a day or two later. Don't be alarmed if your pups vary slightly from the average.

Puppies exhibiting swelling under their sealed eyelids during the first ten days of life may have a conjunctival (the mucous membrane surface that lines the eyelids) infection. It is most often seen immediately before the eyelids part. Those puppies are often restless and sometimes rub at their eyes with their feet. A purulent,

thick, yellow discharge oozes from a tiny aperture between the eyelids, causing the dam to lick at the unopened eyes, cleaning them frequently. To treat:

- Obtain some sterile ophthalmic irrigating solution from the pharmacy.
- Soak a cotton ball or cotton swab with the solution and gently wash both eyes.
- Stroke the eyelids with the soaked cotton upward and downward to encourage the eyelids to part. Do not force them apart with tweezers or swab sticks.
- Repeat the washing four or five times daily.

If the eyelids do not open within a day, consult your veterinarian. The eyelids may rarely require surgical opening, or an antibiotic ointment may be prescribed to squeeze into the opening between the eyelids.

Drug Usage in Neonatal Puppies

The best advice on this subject is to use no drugs without specific knowledge of safety and efficacy of those products. Absorption from newborn puppies' gastrointestinal tracts is not the same as adults. Neonates have little muscle mass, and blood supply to the various organs and muscles differs from that of adults. Body fat is much lower and fluids are much higher in neonates; thus drug distribution is also quite different than in adults.

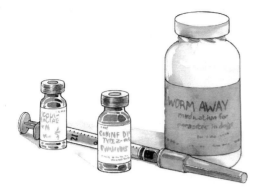

Medicine dosages are critical and vary according to age, size, and health of patient.

The protein makeup of puppies differs significantly from adults, and drugs are metabolized at different rates due to puppies' immature enzyme systems.

In short, don't give puppies drugs without specific veterinary advice and directions that are applicable to the age of the animal on which the drug is being used. Normal dosage levels of drugs for adults might be toxic to young puppies, even when calculated on a weight basis.

Monstra (Developmental Anomalies)

Birth of a fetal monstrum or monster occasionally occurs in most breeds. Monstra (plural of *monstrum*) are newborn animals with congenital anomalies that are greatly pronounced and evident. They include extra heads or duplication of other body parts, absence of extremities or organs, and many other physical abnormalities. Monstra are often stillborn or die shortly after birth but some may survive longer if provided special support.

"Swimmer" puppies or "flat" pups aren't breed specific, but are seen more frequently in bulldogs than in other breeds. They typically lie flat on their abdomens, with their legs extended to each side on the same plane as their bodies. Their ineffective, swimming-like attempts to crawl make them appear like seals out of the water. They can't stand because their legs never approach a vertical position. The condition is also reported in Boston terriers, boxers, cockers, Pekingese, Labrador retrievers, golden retrievers, and other breeds.

Swimmers are sometimes treated by temporarily fastening their hind legs together with tape or bandages. That brings the legs to right angles with their bodies and encourages the pups to try to support weight on them. Some swimmers seem to recover completely and are placed in pet homes, while others retain the flat conformation and can't compete with siblings. Many are destroyed when diagnosed to reduce competition for milk and minimize stress on the dam.

Anasarca (lethal edema) is the term applied to huge puppies that are usually delivered by cesarean section. Also known as water puppies or walrus puppies, they may weigh three or four times more than normal pups in the litter. Water puppies suffer from fluid accumulation under their skins and in their body cavities. They are usually stillborn, although less affected pups may survive. The condition is most prevalent in English bulldogs, and is one of the reasons for routine cesarean sections in that breed.

We have discussed genetic problems such as swimmers, cleft palates, and other congenital and possibly genetically transmitted conditions. While some breeds certainly have their share of genetic problems, too often all hereditary faults are incorrectly identified with purebred dogs. To fully understand reported data, some other facts are needed.

Only about 30 percent of the total dog population of the country represents purebred dogs; however, purebreds (or animals that are phenotypically similar to purebreds) make up 50 to 75 percent of the canine veterinary patients of the country. Therefore, most data reported by veterinarians applies to purebreds.

Neonatal Death

Neonatal death is a painful but necessary topic to cover. About 65 percent of all puppy deaths occur in the first week. According to most sources, dog breeders can expect to lose between 10 and 30 percent of their full-term newborn puppies. Those figures include losses due to poor management, trauma, and

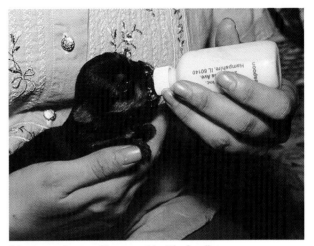
Most puppies readily accept bottle-feeding.

infectious diseases. About half of those newborn deaths are stillborn. Only about 1 percent of all puppy losses occur after weaning.

If your puppy losses approach 15 percent, you should seriously reconsider your breeding program, nutrition, sanitation, and quality of breeding stock.

Infectious diseases do not claim many puppies before weaning today due to the emphasis by conscientious dog breeders on immunization programs. If a bitch is in good health and properly immunized at breeding time, the puppies are usually well protected by colostral antibodies.

Cannibalism

Cannibalism is an infrequent cause of puppy deaths. It is more common in older brood bitches and in those that are overcrowded, nervous, and uncomfortable in their environment. In my experience, cannibalism is rare in home-raised bitches, and is seen more often in those that whelp in noisy, crowded breeding kennels filled with other dogs.

A bitch may eat one or more of her puppies at the time they are born, or she may wait a day or two. Sometimes the entire litter is consumed at birth. One might speculate that cannibalism is more prevalent in the larger, more aggressive breeds, but I saw it as commonly in small breeds. Bitches that cannibalize one litter will usually repeat the activity if the next litter is born under similar conditions. If her whelping environment is stabilized, and she persists in the habit, remove her from your breeding program.

Cannibalistic traits may or may not be hereditary. The same is true for other characteristics relating to a dam's responsibility toward her offspring. Accumulated information on the habits of brood bitches add to our knowledge on this subject every year.

Colostrum

Puppies acquire most of their neonatal immunity through the dam's colostrum (first milk). Little of her immunity to infectious diseases is passed to her puppies before they are born. That critically important colostrum, only produced for the first few days of lactation, is a nutrient-dense milk that also contains high levels of antibodies. Infant puppies' digestive systems are able to absorb those antibodies into their bloodstreams without digesting and destroying them as they would other protein elements. Nutrients found the in bitch's milk can be duplicated fairly well commercially, but no artificial replacer formula compares to colostrum.

Puppies that don't receive colostrum are at risk from infectious diseases and should be raised in a very protected environment. Colostrum banks are invaluable to large canine breeding programs. It can be milked from bitches with small litters, and frozen for future orphan puppies or premature puppies that must be stomach tube-fed.

Technical information that describes sterile collection, qualitative preservation, and trustworthy administration of colostrum is beyond the scope of this book. Information is available to you as a dedicated dog breeder from your veterinarian or a canine reproductive specialist. Be cautious about using home methods without proper information and instruction. Contamination of colostrum with skin and coat bacteria or mastitis organisms can result in sick puppies. Preservation techniques can destroy the antibody content, rendering the colostrum less valuable, and giving you a false sense of security.

Causes of Neonatal Deaths

There are literally dozens of recorded causes of puppy losses before weaning age. The list of causes begins with the dam's poor health, inadequate nutrition, and inferior condition; other causes are associated with puppy depression due to prolonged labor or dystocia.

Poor environmental sanitation, nursery temperature extremes, cannibalism, congenital organ defects, infections, abandonment, and premature births account for other puppy losses. In the absence of proper whelping boxes, large-breed pups are often lost to suffocation from being sat on or laid on by their dams. Puppies born among the folds of blankets and towels sometimes meet the same fate. Large litters may experience losses due to nutritional inadequacy if they are not supplemented.

Accidental deaths are seen when puppies are whelped without benefit of confinement. They crawl about and stray from their nest and are stepped on or killed by other pets in the household.

Fading Pup Syndrome

For no apparent reason, an individual pup's appetite dwindles. It becomes listless, loses weight, and within a few days to a week, it dies. The cause of death is frequently unidentifiable. Over the years, fading or wasting pups' deaths have been attributed to infectious agents, nutritional stresses, infections in the dam, toxemia, and many other suppositions. The condition is more baffling because it can affect one or two pups or the entire litter, and can begin at virtually any age. A great deal of research related to thymus gland influence in the syndrome has been rewarding, but to the best of my knowledge no firm consensus has yet been reached.

The only advice I have to offer if a puppy is suspected of fading is to closely watch its nursing habits or eating habits if it is on solid food. Record its temperature and weigh it twice daily. Compare its temperatures, weights, and habits with others in the litter. Have the pup examined by a veterinarian who has access to your records.

Many neonatal deaths can be avoided by careful kennel management. Puppy survival begins with your choice of strong breeding stock as strong puppies are rarely produced from weak parents. Knowing what to do, how and when to do it, and when to call for help will save puppies! That is not to imply that all competent, knowledgeable breeders wean 100 percent of the pups born to their kennel. It is only to suggest that you now have more control over neonatal deaths than your uninformed counterparts.

Rearing Orphan Puppies

In a worst case scenario, a bitch may die at the time of whelping or shortly thereafter or injury or debilitation might render her unable to nurse and care for her litter. Occasionally, a bitch abandons her litter. In any case, if the dam doesn't take care of her brood, you inherit the chores by default. What do you do? Several questions must first be asked.

Did the puppies nurse from their mother? If so, how long? If they all managed to obtain a few feedings of colostral milk, the risk of death due to nutritional problems and infections are greatly reduced. The nutrient-rich and antibody-filled colostrum is your greatest ally in successfully raising orphans.

Bitches that are healthy but can't or won't voluntarily feed the litter, should be laid in the nursery box to allow the puppies to nurse. If that is not a practical option, take steps to collect and feed her colostrum to them. Collection is easily done with breast pumps obtained from pet supply catalogs or stores. If neither option is possible, ask your veterinarian and officers of local dog clubs to help locate a source of colostrum. Be sure to obtain expert instructions in use of colostrum from an unrelated bitch.

Stomach tube feeding. Your health care professional may wish to instruct you in the art of stomach tube feeding newborn orphans. It is often the best method to administer measured amounts of colostrum to tiny puppies. If colostrum is not available, consult with a veterinarian about the use of gamma globulin injections. They don't take the place of first milk, but may be the next best option for you.

Isolation. Make arrangements to totally isolate the orphans from human and animal society until old enough to be vaccinated. If the puppies received no colostrum, their immunity is practically zero, which means they may receive vaccinations at a younger age than average, but not before they are old enough to produce antibodies themselves. During those critical first few weeks, they are highly susceptible to infectious diseases since they are too young to develop immunity from vaccinations.

If the bitch is alive and not contagious, will she help raise the pups? Even if she has no milk to offer, your duties are significantly reduced if she cleans and cuddles them. Many brood bitches will regain milk production capacity after recovery from disease or injury.

Orphan pups should always be kept together when possible. They will benefit from common body heat, and their personalities will be enhanced from communication with their siblings every day.

Environment Control

Create an orphan nursery from a box or appropriate-sized fiberglass shipping kennel. In large breeds, you might adopt a small room that is easily cleaned. It should provide adequate ventilation and light, but must protect the puppies from drafts and cold. It should be large enough to allow all puppies to stretch out and move about easily, yet small enough to keep them within easy access to one another. You will probably need to change

the nursery accommodations as the puppies grow and become more active and independent.

Floors should be covered with several layers of flat newspapers that are changed at least once daily. When selecting bedding, remember that pups are messy. Old towels or crib blankets that withstand repeated washings are best. Bedding should be changed as often as necessary to keep the pups clean.

Use two or three reliable thermometers in the nursery. One should measure the temperature of bedding immediately over the source of warmth. A second is hung a foot above the floor of the nursery, over the source of warmth, to display the ambient temperature. A third might be placed on the floor well away from the source of warmth.

Most nursery floors are heated to about 90°F (32°C) by means of a heating pad on a low setting, and covered with several layers of blankets or towels. Place the heating pad at one end of the nursery box or area, so that puppies can move away from the heat, if desired. The discussion on page 131 relative to hot water in towel-covered soda bottles applies to nursery heat. They provide three-dimensional sources of warmth, much like the puppies' dam, but it takes time to replenish the hot water every few hours.

The ambient temperature of the nursery should be 75°F (24°C) to 80°F (26.5°C), several degrees

139

Obedience training, both on and off leash, is especially important in large breeds.

lower than the bedding. If kept too warm, it may cause dehydration.

Feeding

Newborn orphan puppies should be bottle-fed four times daily for the first week, then three times daily until they begin eating solid food. Weak or debilitated pups can be fed more often, according to their capacity and needs. Mealtimes should be spaced as equally as possible during a 24-hour period.

Do not feed cows' milk, goats' milk, or similar products. They may be palatable to the puppies, but they do not provide necessary nutrients. Neonatal puppies require no separate water source until eating solid food.

A number of excellent quality bitch milk replacer formulas are available from commercial sources. Carefully read and follow the label directions. If using powdered products, mix them according to directions to ensure that no clumps or foam are present when fed. Be sure to shake liquid product containers well before opening, store excess formula under refrigeration, and stir it well before feeding. Milk replacer should be warmed to body temperature, about 100°F (38°C), before feeding.

Formulas are best fed from commercial canine nursing bottles. Various sizes are available for use in different size puppies. If puppies will not nurse, obtain instructions from your veterinarian for stomach tube feeding. Don't stomach tube feed your puppies to save time and trouble! For healthy pups, stomach tubes are a poor second choice to nursing bottles. The nursing action of puppies is a natural precursor to eating solid food, but it is precluded by persistent stomach tube feeding.

Stimulate Eliminations and Nursing

Before feeding a puppy, hold it in one hand, belly up. (You may want to hold it in a washcloth instead of in your bare hand.) Gently wipe its lower belly and anal area with a small, warm, damp sponge. Stroke the area slowly and firmly for several seconds, imitating the dam's tongue action. Licking stimulates defecation and urination.

After stimulating its eliminations, turn the pup over in your hand and squeeze a drop of milk onto the tip of the bottle nipple. Place the nipple against the pup's muzzle, moving it from side to side. If the puppy doesn't open its mouth and begin to nurse, gently force a finger into its mouth and squeeze a drop or two of milk on its tongue. Then remove your finger while inserting the nipple into its mouth.

Don't be discouraged if puppies fail to nurse on your initial trial. When puppies are first introduced to an artificial source of milk, they often reject it. Wait a few minutes and try again. After a few attempts, you will succeed, and the procedure gets easier with each feeding.

Orphan puppies are easily bottle-fed.

Within a day or two, puppies will respond to your touch and begin searching for the nipple as soon as you lift them from their nest—your surrogate motherhood is established! Hungry puppies that taste formula get the idea quickly and accept a nursing bottle readily.

It is easy to drown puppies by squirting milk into their mouths with syringes. If puppies' tongues do not wrap around a nipple, their swallowing reflexes don't work. Likewise, spoon-feeding neonatal puppies is not a viable option as they have no lapping instinct until they are several weeks old.

To avoid mistakes, record the success of each feeding on the puppies' records as they are fed.

When puppies voluntarily nurse from bottles, do not limit the amount of milk replacer offered.

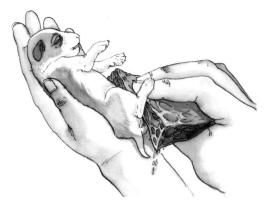

Massage orphan puppies' abdomen to stimulate urination and defecation.

Allow them to take all they want at each feeding. If stomach tube feeding, your instructions will include the amount of food to administer and the frequency. Sometimes more concentrated formulas are given by stomach tube, supplemented intermittently with glucose and electrolyte solutions.

Raising orphan puppies demands particular attention to weight gain and body temperature monitoring. Both should be recorded at least once daily. The character of orphan pups' stools should also be observed and any changes recorded.

When orphan puppies reach three weeks of age, solid food should be offered. Formulas and techniques are discussed later in this chapter. Likewise, if required by breed standards, their dewclaws and tails should be amputated at the same times non-orphan puppies' are done (see page 143).

Dentition

Puppies are born toothless. Their teeth erupt according to their own schedules which vary greatly. The averages given here apply to mid-sized dogs.

- Canines, like humans, have two sets of teeth—deciduous (temporary or milk teeth) and permanents. The first deciduous teeth to erupt are the incisors in the front of the mouth. Those 12 teeth begin to peek through the gums at four to five weeks of age. There are three of them on each side, six on the top and six on the bottom.
- Dogs have four canine teeth, one on either side, top and bottom, just behind the third incisor. They erupt at about the same time as the incisors.
- The 12 premolars erupt about a week later, and are positioned behind the canines, three on each side, top and bottom. They complete the set of 28 deciduous or milk teeth.
- At about 12 weeks of age, the central deciduous incisors begin to loosen and are quickly replaced by permanent teeth. Usually by 16 to 20 weeks of age, all 12 permanent incisors are in place.
- The four permanent canine teeth are often the last to appear, and typically are not visible until about six months of age.
- Permanent premolars begin to erupt at about 16 weeks of age.

There are four on each side, top and bottom, and the rearmost are usually visible by six months of age. Those 16 permanent teeth take the place of the 12 deciduous premolars.

- The two upper molars on each side and three lower molars on each side also begin to appear at about 16 weeks, with the last of the ten erupting at about six months.
- The complete set of 42 permanent teeth is seen in most medium-sized and large breeds of dogs. Variations are common between breeds with toys sometimes having smaller numbers.

Dewclaw Amputation, Tail Docking

Dewclaws

Puppies' front dewclaws anatomically correspond to human thumbs; the difference is in attachment and use. Dewclaws are positioned on the inside of each foreleg, well above the origin of the other four toes. They don't touch the ground and are not used for walking or balance. Some are very loosely attached; others fit tightly against the leg. They are useless appendages that often snag on furniture, or on grass and weeds in the field.

For those reasons, and for appearance, dewclaw amputations are usually done at three to six days

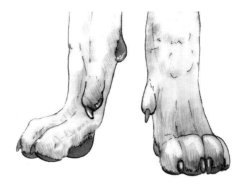

Position of dewclaws on canine adult.

of age. If done too early, bleeding becomes a problem, since the puppies' clotting mechanisms are not adequately developed. Correctly timed, the minor surgery is not terribly painful when proper techniques are followed. Check your breed standard to see if front dewclaw removal and tail docking are required.

Tail Docking

Tail docking is done according to breed standards. If your breed standard requires tail amputation, it should be done at the same time as the dewclaw surgery.

Admittedly, tail docking and dewclaw amputations are sometimes performed by breeders, but I believe you will see many advantages to having the surgery done by a qualified veterinarian. Skin preparation and equipment sterilization is critical. Appropriate equipment and experience using it makes the procedure less painful and faster. Ability to control hemorrhage without insulting delicate puppy tissues is equally essential.

Infections

Infections are common when insufficient attention is paid to sterile surgical techniques. Infected tail or dewclaw wounds are not likely to cause serious systemic illnesses or deaths, but they often result in permanent unsightly scars. There are many professional, surgical techniques that will result in little scarring and smooth-appearing legs.

Some veterinarians allow dewclaw and tail wounds to heal open, that is, without suturing, but I prefer to close the wounds. If sterile technique is used, the wounds heal quicker and smoother when they are closed. Your veterinarian can close the wounds by suturing or with surgical glue. Suture materials vary from absorbable gut or synthetics to nonabsorbable linen, silk, or nylon types, depending on the preference of the surgeon and the size and age of the puppies.

Hind dewclaws are extra toes, usually very loosely attached to the inside of hind legs just above the foot. They are of no use, and are removed from most breeds with a few exceptions (some breeders of giant dogs prefer to leave the hind dewclaws). Check your breed standard.

Solid Food Introduction

At about three weeks of age, most puppies are ready for supplemental feeding of semisolid food. Some breeders use baby food products; others prefer dry puppy foods mixed with warm water. I do not recommend feeding puppies human baby foods packaged in those handy little jars as they often cause diarrhea, even in older puppies. Premium canned foods, fed by themselves, are also a bit rich for three or four-week-old pups in my experience and I prefer to mix dry products with canned, then reduce the mixture to gravy consistency with warm water. Dry premium brands of puppy foods moistened with warm water, without any meat are accepted quickly by aggressive, hungry puppies.

An old formula that still works predates commercial puppy foods. For many years I routinely used and prescribed this starter diet for three or four-week-old pups. Mix ⅓ small

Start feeding solid food by pushing muzzle into soft mixture of puppy food.

curd cottage cheese, ⅓ dry, human infant mixed cereal, and ⅓ cooked and drained hamburger. The three ingredients are thoroughly blended with warm water to the consistency of smooth gravy. Place a saucer with a tablespoonful of the food on the floor and, one by one, gently dip each puppy's muzzle into the food. Usually the puppies will immediately lick their muzzles, taste the food, and search for its source.

After a few days, gradually substitute dry premium puppy food for the infant cereal and continue soaking and mixing it in the same manner. After a few more days, gradually substitute a premium quality canned puppy food for the cottage cheese and hamburger. As soon as they are eating the combination of dry and canned food three times daily, bottle feeding is discontinued. The quantity of solid food mixtures need not be regulated. Allow the puppies to eat all they want. Watch their stools carefully during this period. If very soft or liquid stools are seen, identify the pup involved and restrict its consumption for a few days.

When solid food is regularly consumed, leave a pan of dry puppy food in the nursery for free-choice eating. (If the dam has access to the nursery at this time, use a creep feeder for the puppies' dry food [see Creep Feeding, page 146].) Some may begin to eat it immediately, others may not be interested for a week or two. By the time the litter is six weeks old, all should be eating solid food regularly.

Chapter 13

Weaning

Many factors should be considered when choosing the best weaning time for puppies. Seeking a weaning age that applies to every puppy from every bitch in your kennel is a futile endeavor. I have heard breeders say they always take a bitch away from her litter when the pups are five weeks old, or some other specific age. Inexperienced veterinarians, looking for a quick and easy answer to an often asked question, remark that all pups should be weaned at a particular age. Don't believe it!

Experienced dams, especially with their second and third litters, may wean puppies without consulting their owners. When puppies begin eating solid food, the character of their stools changes significantly. That seems to be the stimulus for a bitch to start the weaning process. She may first cease to clean up their feces. Then she allows them to nurse only when her glands are very full. Within a week, she only nurses them once or twice a day.

After weaning, some bitches continue to train and play with their puppies until they are sold and leave the premises. Dams tolerate their own puppies' mischievous nuisance behavior when similar actions from strangers are immediately rejected. One of the admirable characteristics of fine brood bitches is the propensity to attend to and discipline their litters long after they have stopped feeding them.

Techniques and formulas for starting puppies on solid food was covered in the previous chapter (see Solid Food Introduction, pages 144–145). When solid food is introduced, free access to fresh drinking water must also be supplied. Invest in some spill-proof water bowls and always keep them on an impervious, washable surface.

Dams will compete with their broods for their tasty new puppy food. That usually mandates separation of pups from mothers during their feeding times. Puppies should be eating three meals of semisolid food each day by five to six weeks of age.

Creep Feeding

When dry puppy food is left for a litter, and their mother has access to the nursery, she will probably gobble up their food as soon as she spots it. To solve that problem, I suggest you build a creep feeder.

How to Build

I found that a sturdy plastic basket about two feet (61 cm) square worked wonderfully. I cut a four-inch (10 cm)-wide and six-inch (15 cm)-deep notch out of the top of each side. The crate was then turned upside down over a pan of dry puppy food. Each notch was large enough for four-week-old puppies to squeeze through, but small enough to prevent entry of the dam's muzzle. The result was a ventilated cover for puppy food that gave the pups free access to it. I soon discovered that it must be fastened to the floor to prevent our malamute bitch from tipping it over. For less powerful dogs, a weight on the basket serves the same purpose.

Eating habits are relative. Precocious pups may begin eating solid food at three weeks, especially if the litter is large, competition is great, and milk supply is limited. Conversely, it takes a lot of coaxing to interest puppies in solid food if they are fat and happy, from a small litter, with a heavy milk-producing dam.

Feeding the pups apart from the dam is the first stage of weaning the litter. I don't recommend total separation from the dam or physically preventing them from nursing before six weeks of age. She should be allowed to visit them whenever their food is not available to her.

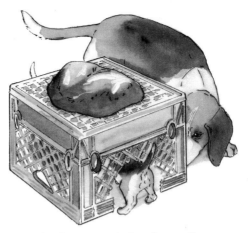

Creep feeding prevents dam from eating puppies' food.

If feeding the dam free choice, and if the puppies have access to a premium dry dog food, they may nibble at it between their regular meals. When pups are seen eating dry food, they also require a constant source of water.

Emotional Maturity

Advanced, well-developed puppies that begin eating their dam's food at a very early age are not necessarily ready to wean. An aggressive appetite is only one sign of maturity. Weaning often implies sale of a puppy, and relates not only to its diet, but also to physical removal from siblings and maternal influence. Weaning puppies before they are emotionally ready can affect their personalities.

From birth, puppies sleep huddled together in a bunch. They are only secure and comfortable when

Independent playing is a sign that weaning time is near.

nursing or when in physical contact with their siblings. One of the first noticeable signs of maturity is when that characteristic diminishes, and puppies begin to sleep apart from one another. About that same time, individuals will be seen wandering about the nursery, perhaps chewing on a toy or playing with another puppy independently from the others. Independence is another determining characteristic of weaning readiness.

The only general weaning rule we wish to promulgate is to choose a weaning age after serious evaluation of the physical and mental maturity of individual puppies. Human bonding and the dam's condition and attitude are equally important components of the picture. I believe there is no particular age at which all pups should be weaned. Puppies of some breeds develop more rapidly than others. Puppies from large litters usually can be weaned earlier than those from small litters.

All puppies from the litter do not necessarily mature physically or emotionally at the same rate. Watch for adventurous, clever fellows that scout the nursery, sleep apart from their siblings, play roughly with one another, compete for food, and come to you each time you approach. Those individuals are reaching weaning time.

Socialization

Don't be in a hurry—puppies must also be socialized, and it doesn't happen overnight. The human bonding process begins when their eyes first open. Three weeks to three months of age is the most crucial time for bonding. As a conscientious dog breeder, you have an important obligation to handle your pups regularly at that impressionable time. Puppies of any age that aren't comfortable in human society are not ready to separate from their dam and siblings. It is important to try to place puppies in their new homes some time before three months of age. Older pups and adults certainly bond to new families, but the process takes longer. Canine trust and obedience is more easily learned before three months.

The Final Test

As implied, the final decision for weaning time should be left to individual puppies. When a hearty, independent six-week-old (or older) puppy is taken from the nest, and it readily plays with you, follows you about, comes to you, and cries when you put it back in the nursery, it is ready to wean. When it seems to prefer human company to that of its siblings, it is ready for a new home.

The Weaning Diet

By the time your litter is weaned, the puppies are eating three meals of premium quality dry puppy food, mixed with water and perhaps a bit of premium canned food (see Solid Food Introduction, page 144). They have free access to dry puppy food and water as well. Don't make any further dietary changes except increases in quantities fed. Litters of more than three should be separated into smaller groups when eating their moist meals to discourage overindulgence of the heartiest eaters, and to help assure that all get their equal shares.

Diet supplementation with vitamins and minerals is not necessary, providing their food is formulated for growing puppies (see discussion on nutrition and dog food labeling, page 25), based on feeding trials. If deficiencies are suspected, or breed growth patterns have been identified that require supplementation, consult with your veterinary nutritional adviser. It can be very dangerous to arbitrarily add mineral supplements to puppies' diets, and excessive amounts of some vitamins are also contraindicated.

Don't feed your puppies cows' milk, especially not at weaning time. Even after taking all the precautions we have discussed, weaning is a stressful season in puppies' lives. Milk, rich foods, table scraps, and meat products are likely to cause diarrhea that further stresses the puppies.

It is important to keep written records of specific foods your puppies are fed, the amounts, and times of feeding. A copy of that record should accompany each puppy as it goes into a new home. Make sure the new owner realizes that dietary changes, other than gradual increases in quantities, can be dangerous and should be made watchfully and very gradually.

Prospective Buyers

A word of caution is in order regarding prospective buyers. You will no doubt have friends and neighbors interested in your puppies. Breeders may wish to consider them as well, especially if your breeding stock is superior quality. Others answer advertisements or are referred to you.

Take great care when allowing people to handle your puppies before they are vaccinated. Some diseases, notably the upper respiratory varieties, are highly contagious and can be transmitted by human hands.

If someone answers your ad and shows up at your door, ask if they handled other puppies before coming to your home or kennel. If so, I suggest you ask them to look at the pups from a distance of several feet, and come back again another time to physically handle them. You may lose a sale if an uninformed prospective buyer is offended, but that is of minor importance compared to the health of the entire litter.

Interviewing Prospective Buyers

Our accepted premise is that pet stewardship is one of our obligations. That includes placing your new puppies into homes that also accept that philosophy. Many families have plenty of money to buy dogs, but no interest in caring for them.

There are some things you can do to ensure that the homes you find for your puppies are good ones. Ask questions about the prospective owners' housing facilities and intentions. If they want to breed dogs, be sure they have sufficient knowledge about the process. If they want a pet, be sure they intend to have the animal neutered at an appropriate age. Be especially wary of those who wish to purchase a puppy as a gift.

If possible, discuss these points with prospective buyers on the telephone before inviting them to see your puppies, and before actually offering them for sale.

Consider using a contract that assures neutering of pets, returning puppies to you if new owners can't keep them, and declaration of the breeding or showing quality of pup-

pies purchased for those purposes. Other clauses relative to health and immunization can be included. It is critical to emphasize the importance of limiting promiscuous puppy production, and the owners' financial and moral obligation to provide safe, stable, loving environments for new puppies.

Most all-breed clubs and specialty dog clubs have sample contracts and instructions for members. Look them over and adapt them to your situation.

Physical Examinations and Vaccinations

At about six weeks of age, before they are offered for sale, puppies should be taken to the veterinarian. Always call in advance to be sure that sufficient time is reserved for physical examination of the litter. Even puppies that were examined previously should be reexamined at this age. Your veterinarian will go over each pup in turn and will likely administer their first vaccinations.

It is impractical to discuss specific immunization schedules in this book. Excellent immunity is almost certain from some vaccines, while other products are less predictable. Stay informed by asking about the agents being administered. Learn what vaccine is being given, the product's efficacy, its possible side effects, signs of reaction, and what to do about them if they are seen. Veterinary clinicians in your local area are aware of diseases that are endemic and those that have been recently identified. They can advise you about which vaccines are appropriate for your operation. Certain breeds are known to be more susceptible to some diseases than others. Vaccination programs should be tailored to meet the breeders' particular needs in their specific localities.

Most vaccines contain living, freeze-dried microorganisms that require mixing with a sterile solution contained in another vial. Effectiveness of vaccines depends on attention to many details. Seemingly minor mistakes in handling vaccines may be costly in the end.

Biologics are kept refrigerated from the time produced until administered to dogs. Manufacturers of veterinary biologics usually ship their vaccines directly to veterinary clinics and hospitals. Other biologics, however, travel from a manufacturer to a national distributor, a regional or local distributor, then to a catalog merchant or pet supply store. The more hands through which those sensitive vaccines travel, the higher the risk is for handling errors.

I recently shopped canine vaccines sold over the counter. I was appalled to find instructions for use of a cat biologic packaged with a dog vaccine. I found a vial of sterile diluent from one manufacturer packaged with a freeze-dried canine

Before going to new homes, puppies should be examined and vaccinated.

vaccine from a different manufacturer. I discovered vaccines packaged and sold with no inserts or directions, and others with directions that had been reproduced on a copy machine. Those obviously sloppy marketing techniques do not necessarily reflect the efficacy of the vaccines when they left the manufacturer, but they should alert us to potential mistakes that can be made behind the scenes. Don't gamble with your dogs' lives; they depend on your wisdom.

Vaccine administration is another area in which mistakes are commonly made by those who are not knowledgeable and trained in handling biologics. Modified live virus vaccines (MLV) are living products, as their name implies. To be effective, they must be administered as living products to healthy animals.

Dam turns to assist a puppy emerging from her birth canal. Pup is still contained within its amniotic sac.

Example: I once worked with a disease outbreak in a large working dog kennel. Two new young adult dogs joined the kennel and the next day both began vomiting and were noticeably ill.

Canine infectious hepatitis (CAV-1) (see page 154) was diagnosed. The new dogs were isolated and

As soon as the pup is born, the dam begins to clean the amniotic membranes from its head.

treated, but unfortunately both died in a few days. About eight days later, signs of CAV-1 developed in many of the kennel's puppies and one or two adults.

Upon review, the kennel's vaccination program seemed adequate, but the animals obviously did not receive protective immunity. The dogs were thought to be in good health when vaccinated by the owner, but none were actually examined. The vaccine used was excellent quality, but mishandling of equipment and vaccine was a distinct possibility. About ten puppies and six or seven young adults died, and several animals that recovered had permanent organ damage. It was a sad and expensive lesson, one that was not repeated.

In my experience, lack of understanding of biological properties, techniques, equipment, and principals of immunization can get a do-it-yourself breeder into a world of trouble. Don't let false economics lead you into a death trap.

Some Diseases Preventable by Vaccination

Vaccination schedules are individually designed and must consider colostral immunity, probability of exposure, puppy health, age, and stress factors. Vaccination comments are here offered here in very general terms and do not apply to all situations.

Keep in mind that neonatal puppy immunity is initiated by antibodies obtained from the colostrum in the dam's milk the first few days of life. Those antibodies have a limited life span and gradually diminish as the puppies mature. Live vaccines administered too early may not be effective because of existing antibody levels. If administered too late, the window of opportunity for exposure to disease is enlarged. Timing is critical and should be discussed with your veterinarian.

Dam continues to lick and roll the puppy, drying it, and stimulating its respiration.

Canine Distemper

In spite of modern effective vaccines, canine distemper is still a significant threat to young puppies. Its mortality rate, lack of cure, and easy transmission make it one of the most important canine diseases. Distemper is truly a neurological disease, but affected puppies may exhibit many symptoms including coughing, ocular and nasal discharge, pneumonia, appetite reduction, weight loss, weakness, staggering, diarrhea, convulsions, and others.

Differentiating it from other contagious puppy maladies is a challenge early in the course of the disease. When contracted by very young, unvaccinated pups, it often causes sudden death. Others may seem to respond to various treatments, and survive, only to succumb to convulsions and paralysis at a later date. Even those that miraculously live through the disease are often scarred by tooth enamel deficiencies

and permanent neurological signs such as twitching of extremities.

The first of a series of distemper vaccinations is given at about six weeks of age, and the vaccine is usually combined with other vaccines. Annual boosters are required.

Dam severs the umbilical cord and eats the placenta.

Wiping an orphan neonate's belly to stimulate defecation and urination.

CAV-1

Canine infectious hepatitis is another highly contagious, incurable, fatal disease of dogs. Now known by the initials CAV-1 (which stands for canine adenovirus, type 1), it is a systemic disease that ultimately severely damages the liver. Symptoms often mimic those of

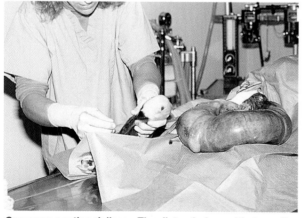

Cesarean-section delivery. The distended, gravid uterus lies on the surgical drape.

distemper and in very young pups sudden death is sometimes seen.

Vaccines are highly effective in preventing CAV-1, and are included in combination products with distemper and leptospirosis. A series of vaccinations is begun at or after six weeks, with annual boosters.

Leptospirosis

Leptospirosis can also be fatal. Unlike distemper and CAV-1, its vaccine is a killed immunizing agent. Leptospirosis is not a viral disease, but is caused by a spirochete somewhat resembling bacteria. It is also contagious to other dogs and to humans and is transmitted by urine from infected animals. Treatment of a lepto infection can be effective, but permanent kidney damage resulting from an infection can be very serious. Leptospirosis vaccine is usually combined with distemper and hepatitis products.

Parvo and Corona Viruses

Parvo virus and corona viruses are among the more recently documented contagious and often fatal canine diseases. Causing severe diarrhea, vomiting, dehydration, and depression, they are especially devastating to puppies. Supportive therapy sometimes improves the prognosis, but in young animals, sudden death is common. Vaccinations are usually given at the same time as the other biologics, at or shortly after six weeks of age, with annual boosters also required. New immunizing agents are being introduced regularly and vaccination schedules change with each new product. Consult with your veterinary practitioner about the use of those products.

Parainfluenza and Bordetella

A pair of respiratory conditions, parainfluenza virus and Bordetella (a bacterial organism), round out the diseases against which your puppies should be vaccinated at an early age. Both diseases cause coughing, fever, loss of appetite, and depression. Unheeded, secondary pneumonia can result and both can be fatal. They are highly contagious and are easily spread by aerosol transmission.

Epidemics are seen in situations where dogs are housed in close contact with others, such as in boarding or breeding kennels. One cough or sneeze from an infected dog, and all dogs in the room are exposed. Though both diseases have a lower fatality rate than some of the previously discussed diseases, they deserve serious consideration in your vaccination program.

Vaccines include intranasal types, and are often less predictable than others, but they are improving. Because of recent advances in vaccine research, I advise you to consult with your local veterinarian about Bordetella or parainfluenza vaccines.

Rabies

Rabies is preventable by vaccination, and most, if not all, states

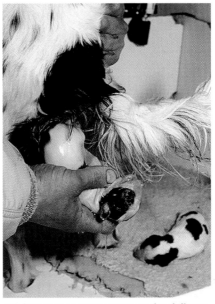

If it becomes necessary to assist delivery, grasp the pup's shoulders and apply gentle traction downward.

require that all dogs be vaccinated. Most contemporary rabies vaccines are highly effective killed products with an extremely low incidence of side effects.

Rabies vaccines are usually given later than the others discussed earlier. Many communities require canine rabies vaccinations at three months of age, and they are rarely given before that time. Many cities, towns, and counties have ordinances or laws that require rabies vaccinations to be administered by or under the direction of licensed, U.S.D.A.-accredited veterinarians. Those laws are made to address the public health significance of the disease.

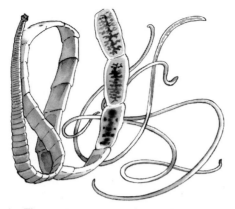

The most common endoparasites: round-worm (R) and tapeworm (L).

Parasites

Intestinal Parasites

Intestinal parasites, especially ascarids (roundworms), hookworms, and coccidiosis, are rarely fatal, but can seriously affect the general health and vitality of puppies. Your bitch was checked for worms before she was bred, and probably once again while pregnant. Even if her tests were negative, the puppies can still be infested by their dam.

Roundworm larvae can remain hidden in cysts in females' tissues throughout the dogs' lives. During pregnancy, larva migrate from those cysts into fetuses, and remain in their livers or lungs until birth. Then they continue migration, and develop in the puppies' intestines, where they mature and produce eggs. Roundworm eggs in feces are the sources of infestation for other dogs (and possibly under certain rare circumstances to children), and are found upon microscopic examination of infested puppies' stools.

Reservoirs for rabies infection are found in carnivores such as skunks, raccoons, coyotes, bats, and other wildlife. Exposure potential for urban, indoor, backyard pets is low, but possible. Since this incurable and fatal disease can be transmitted to humans and all other warm-blooded animals, great emphasis is placed on rabies control.

Details of other intestinal parasites' life cycles are too involved to be addressed here; however, a composite stool sample from your litter of puppies should be taken to your veterinarian when they are examined, at or shortly before, weaning time.

If parasite ova (eggs) are found in a fecal sample, your veterinarian will prescribe an appropriate medication for treatment. If you are administering the medication yourself, be aware that worm medica-

Tapeworm life cycle when flea is secondary host.

tions are types of poisons, so be meticulous in calculating dosages, and carefully follow the label directions. You can cause serious illnesses by allowing puppies to consume excessive amounts of many worm medications. If an infested pup is missed in the worm treatment, it will reinfest the litter.

Never fall into the "old standby" trap—an over-the-counter product you previously used successfully on another dog is not necessarily safe or effective for use in puppies, even at reduced doses. Different medications are prescribed for different parasites. There is no such thing as a catch-all worm medication that is both safe and effective for all intestinal parasites. Many of the older products that still claim a place in the market cause damage to internal organs, especially the liver. Newer products are available that produce no dangerous side effects.

An equally perilous procedure is to "worm" all puppies, whether or not a parasite infestation has been diagnosed. Would you swallow a poison of any kind that might not be needed? Why would you consider the same for your puppies? Even if you use a safe product and follow label directions carefully, in the absence of a diagnosed infestation, your time and medication are wasted. There is no excuse for doing something well that shouldn't be done at all.

There are many other canine parasites that can affect puppies, details of which are beyond the scope of this book; however, a few should be mentioned in passing to alert you to their existence.

Heartworms

Heartworm disease, spread by mosquitoes, can and should be prevented. Follow your veterinarian's advice relative to the age to begin preventative medications, safest products to use, and schedule. The disease doesn't occur universally, and preventative medication is not indicated if the disease is not endemic in your area and if your dog doesn't travel to endemic areas.

Skin Parasites

Dermatological problems such as fungus (ringworm) and mite infestations (mange) are often seen in

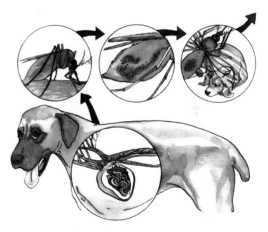

Heartworm life cycle.
1. Adults live inside dog's heart
2. Mosquitoes suck larvae from dog's veins
3. Larvae undergo biological changes inside mosquito
4. Mosquito transmits infective larvae to susceptible dog

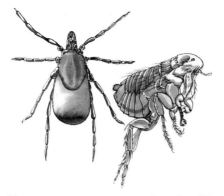

The most common ectoparasites: flea (R) and tick (L).

before infestations can be effectively treated. Skin scrapings examined under a microscope will identify the organism responsible for mange lesions. Examination of ear wax will identify ear mites. Either skin scrapings or cultures are used to identify fungal infections.

Don't rely on a catch-all mange dip or ringworm salve to cure puppy skin diseases. They may create new problems while doing nothing toward solving the initial one.

weanling puppies. The most common mange mites are *Cheyletiella, Demodex, Psoroptes*, and *Sarcoptes.* Another mite, *Otodectes,* may parasitize ears of both cats and dogs. As with other parasites, a definitive diagnosis must be made

Ticks and Fleas

Ticks and fleas are more common in adult dogs that range in kennel runs or backyards, but they can infest a litter of puppies. If those parasites are diagnosed, be sure to follow a treatment program that uses only products proven safe in young animals. Do not use dips, sprays, powders, medicated collars, or other drugs without specific label directions for puppies.

Records

Be sure to record the names of the products used, dates administered, and the dates boosters are due. That record should be kept current, and given to buyers as the puppies are placed in new homes. Those records should contain the results of fecal examinations, parasite infestations and their treatments, and all other medications prescribed or administered.

Flea life cycle.

Chapter 14

The Reproductive Life of Brood Bitches

The breeding, pregnancy, whelping, nursing, and weaning went beautifully. Your litter of beautiful puppies is bringing joy to six happy families. It was an exciting and wonderful experience that you are anxious to repeat, but, before planning the next breeding, ask yourself a few questions.

What is your primary purpose for ownership of the bitch? Does her health claim a high priority in your plans? Is she a pet or a show dog? Did she produce puppies that are excellent representatives of the breed? Was the breeding, pregnancy, whelping, and lactation uncomplicated? Is she a good mother? Were her puppies healthy and strong? Were they placed in show homes, or were they sold or given away as pets? In other words, examine your motives for breeding the bitch again.

If she presented problems at any phase, they may be repeated with future litters. If she produced deformed puppies, mismarked or otherwise less than desirable quality pups, the potential is there for similar deficiencies in future offspring. Unless her puppies were outstanding and in high demand, it may be time to retire her from the breeding program. If she breezed through the process and you had no difficulty finding suitable homes for the pups, you may elect to repeat the breeding.

If you decide to breed her again, there are probably many questions in your mind, such as: When will bitches show signs of proestrus following delivery? How often can or should they be bred? Should they be rested between pregnancies? How many litters can I expect to raise from a well-conditioned brood animal? At what age should breeding stock be retired?

Next Estrous Cycle

Bitches that are sound and healthy, in excellent nutritional condition, and well exercised, will probably begin proestrus on their usual schedules. Uncomplicated breeding, pregnancy, and lactation do not necessarily change the timing of bitches' estrous cycles. If a female displays proestrus every

Afghan puppies taking the opportunity to fill their stomachs.

seven months before she is bred, she will probably repeat proestrus bleeding about five months after whelping unless delayed by poor nutrition, extended lactation, or other stress factors.

Many different repeat-breeding schedules are devised by dog breeders to maximize the reproductive potential of their fine brood bitches. Some commercial operations and puppy farms breed all bitches every time they will stand for a male. That may be an economically sound practice for those who are in the dog breeding business to produce puppies for pet shop markets but it is questionable at best in my opinion. I find it difficult to accept the premise that top-quality offspring are obtained from fatigued dams, and I do not encour-

age that type of schedule under any circumstances.

If your brood bitch is a show winner but also a family member, you no doubt want to protect her health and maximize her comfortable life. Her puppy production is secondary to her value as a pet, but her excellent puppies are easily placed in good homes and remain in demand. Using that postulation, I offer the following advice.

Allow her to rest during the first heat after whelping. If in excellent condition, she may be bred again on the following heat. During the resting period, keep her well exercised, lean, and athletic. Following her next whelping, skip the next estrus and, if ready, breed her on the following heat. An every-other heat breeding program will minimize the stress on your valuable brood bitch.

Example: If a bitch reaches her first proestrus period at eight months of age, her cycle is seven months, and she is first bred when 15 months old, she will have the opportunity of raising four or five litters of puppies during her expected reproductive life of about six years.

If her exhibition career is actively pursued, her reproductive life may be limited to one or two litters. Most animals require a rest of nearly a year before coats and conditioning reach a competitive level. Considering the overabundance of puppies available in the world today, that's not all bad!

If no health problems occur at an earlier time, brood bitches should be retired by six or seven years of age. If breeding complications of any kind occurred, early retirement is prudent.

Although menopause does not occur in canines, brood bitches' reproductive lives end much earlier than those of males. Usually, by six years of age, a bitch has passed her production peak. She continues to cycle, exhibits standing heat, and often conceives when bred. As she ages, puppy resorption is more common, her puppies are often larger in size and smaller in number, and dystocias can occur more frequently.

Uterine Infections

Prolonged labor that accompanies dystocia, and decreased uterine tissue viability seem to increase the probability of uterine infections. Metritis (see page 119) and pyometra (see page 71) occur more commonly in aged intact females. Those infectious diseases are sometimes fatal in young and middle aged bitches, but their danger is multiplied many times in old animals.

False Pregnancy

False pregnancy (pseudocyesis) (see page 64) seems to be more prevalent in older bitches. Although it is a normal and non-pathological condition, it is often a great nuisance. It is usually accompanied by engorged mammary glands that may be painful and are susceptible to infection. Mastitis is seen more frequently in older bitches, and it becomes more significant with age.

Mammary Tumors

Human breast cancer is in the news every day. The incidence of canine mammary cancer is at least three times greater per capita than in women. Mammary tumors comprise nearly half of all canine tumor cases, and at least half of those are malignant. Mammary cancer cells often metastasize to the lymph glands of the region, and sometimes to internal organs.

Mammary tumors may occur at any age, but are rare under two years, more common over six years, and with greatest frequency in 10- or 11-year-old bitches. Surgery is indicated in virtually all mammary tumors. Total mastectomies of affected glands are preferred, and only rarely is it prudent to perform "lumpectomies." Consider that the bitch has 12 mammary glands, each of which can develop tumors and require mastectomy. In spite of the risk, multiple mastectomies are sometimes necessary.

The most influential factor in mammary tumor development seems to be the number of estrous cycles a bitch experiences before she is spayed. If spayed at or before puberty, the risk is negligible. Each time she comes in heat, her predisposition for tumors increases.

Those tumors tend to grow slowly at first, initially noticed as pea-sized or marble-sized nodules. Then, almost overnight, they are enormous. Uninformed owners may not recognize the cause or consequences of the growths, and they are shocked when the full picture is painted by a veterinary clinician.

Treatment

To prevent or minimize occurrence of malignancies in remaining glands, an ovariohysterectomy (spay) should be performed before or at the time mastectomy is done.

I have repeatedly experienced the nightmare of six or seven mammary glands containing malignant tumors, each the size of my fist, in a ten-year-old intact bitch. The only feasible therapy is multiple mastectomies in conjunction with ovariohysterectomy to prevent future tumors in the remaining glands. Extended anesthesia is required, the old bitch's strength and vitality is compromised, recuperation from the extensive surgery is long, stressful, and uncomfortable. Yet there are no options but to operate or euthanize the patient. Fortunately, with adequate support, most patients recover.

Spay Operations for Retired Bitches

Ultimately, the best advice for brood bitch owners is to retire her before the serious maladies of age begin to show up. When the decision to retire her from brood bitch duties is made, schedule an ovariohysterectomy. Nothing is gained by procrastination if she is in good health—it never gets easier or safer by waiting.

Spay operations in older females are somewhat more difficult to perform, and there are slightly higher risks involved than in young animals. Surgical risks are minor compared to the risks of pyometra, ovarian cysts and tumors, and mammary cancer, all of which plague older intact females. *Ovariohysterectomy is the best insurance policy you can buy for your retired brood bitch.*

Spaying Considerations

First, spay operations are not the same as tubal ligations. "Tying the tubes" of intact bitches will certainly stop reproduction, but it does nothing to stop estrous cycles and prevent the many complications that arise from them.

Likewise, various contraceptive procedures don't take the place of ovariohysterectomy. Injections or oral tablets to prevent heats, plastic diapers, and intravaginal devices intended to prevent breeding are available, but they are *not* a substitute for spaying.

Ovariohysterectomy, or spaying, refers to the total surgical removal of both ovaries and the uterus. It is probably the most frequent surgery performed in small animal veterinary practices. Safety is relative to the condition of the dog and competency of the surgeon. The operation is slightly different in every dog, and surgical technique is modified as indicated for each patient.

Spaying Young Bitches

We have discussed spaying retired brood bitches, but more needs to be said about options and impacts of spaying a bitch at other times of life. No book on canine reproduction is complete without mention of those considerations.

The time-honored optimum age to spay a pet is six months, before her first heat. When done at that age, she never shows signs of proestrus bleeding and physiologically, she remains in a perpetual stage of anestrus.

Before her first heat, surgical risk is minimal, the operation is easy to perform, and usually the cost of surgery is the lowest. When spayed at six months of age, mammary tumors and other reproductive-hormone related diseases are avoided for life.

Risks of Spaying

Age constitutes a minor risk factor in strong and healthy bitches up to four or five years. After that age, each year brings with it new risks to be addressed.

Some breeds present higher risks than others. Risks are highest in brachycephalic breeds such as English bulldogs, Pekingese, and Boston terriers. Those risks are related to their skull and facial conformations that result in compromised airways. Precautions are taken in veterinary surgeries to minimize the risks associated with those and other breeds.

Any abdominal surgery in obese animals present higher risks than lean and athletic dogs. Anesthesia may also be complicated in fat dogs as longer incisions are necessary to accommodate the fatty structures being removed. Sutures do not hold as well in fatty tissues, and healing time is often prolonged.

Spaying a young pregnant bitch involves some increased risk, but it is minimal if carefully timed. When a pet is unintentionally bred, ovariohysterectomy is often the safest and most agreeable way to terminate the pregnancy.

Spay Myths

Spayed dogs all get fat, right? Wrong! *Dogs are fat because their dietary intake exceeds their caloric needs.* There are many reasons for obesity, including hormonal imbalances, gluttony, lack of exercise, and hereditary predisposition. Rich foods, overfeeding, table scraps, and treats all contribute to obesity. There certainly may be an association between spaying and obesity, but it is not a cause-and-effect relationship. There is no more excuse for obesity in spayed bitches than in intact bitches.

Spaying a female prevents or removes stresses we have discussed in this book that are related to the reproductive cycle. With those energy-demanding stresses removed, a spayed bitch requires fewer calories than before surgery. If her caloric intake is not adjusted to accommodate her reduced requirements, obesity will result.

Pets are effective beggars. They can con a cookie out of the best of us. Yet how many of us reduce our pets' daily dog food allotment when we feed her a cookie? Is the dog or the owner responsible for fat dogs?

Dog food packages have feeding instructions that do not fit the metabolism of every dog in the world. Active, energy-burning dogs require more calories than "couch potatoes." Nervous dogs are less apt to be obese than those with laid-back personalities. Don't feed your spayed pet according to bag directions; feed her according to her need. Keep her lean and active.

Spaying Working Dogs

Virtually all guide dogs are spayed or castrated at or before puberty—rarely do you see a fat seeing eye dog. The reason is simple. Organizations that raise and train those dogs apply strict dietary controls on them, and those controls are perpetuated by their sightless owners. A fat dog does not perform as well as an athletic one.

Some of the best gun dogs I know are spayed females. They are often kenneled; hence, their food intakes are easily controlled. They are active, energetic working dogs, and they are always ready for the field when the duck or pheasant season opens. Bitches in heat obviously can't be used in open fields, and it is virtually impossible to regulate estrous cycles so they will only come into season when the quail are out of season.

Very Early Spaying and Castration

Because of the overpopulation of unwanted, stray dogs, new interest is surfacing regarding very early castration and spaying. The surgery can be performed as early as 6 to 12 weeks of age. Studies of early neutering indicate that it is a viable option.

The reasons cited for delaying surgery until six months old, or close to puberty, are relative to the adverse effects early surgery might possibly have on them as adults. Abnormal bone formation is predicted, anesthetic risks are feared, perpetual immature behavior is expected, and infantile genitalia is thought to be a health factor.

Those objections to very early spaying and castration seem to fall into shadows in light of recent research. Virtually no health differences were noted between puppies that were spayed or castrated prior to puberty compared to those that were surgically altered at or after puberty. Growth rates and physical development, personalities, and surgical safety did not differ.

The American Veterinary Medical Association embraces the concept of early spaying and castration of dogs in animal shelters. I believe it will be a trend in the future.

Whether recent interest and research in early spaying and castration will have a significant effect on purebred dog breeding is problematical. I can appreciate that such procedures might give a conscientious breeder positive control over which puppies are able to enter the gene pool of the breed. The majority of every litter is of pet quality. At present, the only assurance a breeder has that pets won't be used in breeding programs is a handshake or signature on a document. Neither are likely to hold up in court.

Although I am not promoting prepuberty spaying or castration at the present time, it is not too soon to discuss it with your veterinarian. It might also stimulate an active discussion in dog club meetings.

The Reproductive Life of Stud Dogs

Males' reproductive lives may extend beyond death. Contemporary methods of canine semen storage enables us to collect semen from dogs and preserve it for use in bitches in the future. Natural breeding is possible for many eight-year-old males and some even older. Depending on the breed and condition, small and medium-sized dogs often sire normal litters long past their dog show careers.

There is no particular reason to stop using a stud, providing he receives a complete physical examination with the beginning of each breeding year.

The greatest determining factor for the life of a stud dog is his quality and the quality of his offspring. If he is an excellent representative of the breed and produces even higher quality puppies when bred to outstanding bitches, he should be used as long as practical. Conversely, if he is not stamping quality excellence on his puppies, it is time for his retirement.

A stud dog's influence on a breed may be a hundred times greater than that of a brood bitch's. She may produce two to six litters of puppies in her lifetime. He can produce ten times that number every year. No animal deserves to be considered as a stud dog unless he proves his quality by his offspring.

Chapter 15

Registration, Pedigrees, and Titles

Purebred dogs may be registered by any of several canine registries. Each has its own rules and policies. The American Kennel Club (AKC), registering about one million dogs a year since 1970, is the largest and probably oldest U.S. kennel club. The AKC, founded in 1884, is not a regulatory agency, but a nonprofit organization dedicated to the welfare and advancement of purebred dogs.

The AKC does not license kennels or individual dog breeders, but does train and license dog show judges. The six events that are held under AKC rules include conformation dog shows, obedience trials, tracking tests, field trials, hunting tests, and herding tests.

Standards of all recognized breeds are maintained by the registry. The AKC registers 137 breeds that are separated into seven groups for the purpose of exhibition. Those groups include: Sporting, Hound, Working, Terrier, Toy, Non-sporting, and Herding.

Several breeds are exhibited by varieties. Those include beagles that are shown in either of two size varieties; collies that are shown in one of two coat textures; bullterriers that are shown in either of two coat colors; and others.

Litter Registration

Facts from various AKC documents were used for the following discussion. Other registries' policies and rules may vary, but the principles are the same.

When a litter is born, the owners of both sire and dam complete and sign a *Litter Registration Application* form (available at no cost from the AKC). That form specifies the number of living males and females in the litter, the date of birth, registration numbers and names of both sire and dam, date of mating, and the full names and addresses of sire's and dam's owners. Witnesses to the breeding, information relative to artificial or natural breeding and a rule compliance clause are also included on the form.

Puppy Registration

The application form, together with an appropriate fee, is sent to the registry. When received, the

AKC issues a litter kit to the dam's owner. It includes blue-colored, partially completed application forms for each of the puppies. Preprinted data on the blue slip "puppy registration papers" includes date of birth, parents' names and registration numbers, and litter registration number. One of those blue slips accompanies each puppy as sold.

Names

The new owner completes the blue form, listing the sex of the pup, its color, date purchased, and their own name and address. The puppy may also be named on the blue slip, and once a dog's name is registered, it can't be changed. Advise new owners to give careful consideration to their dog's name. The AKC invites complex names, so as to better identify the dog—simple names like Rex or Buddy just won't do!

Names are limited to 25 letters, and two different names must be submitted. There are many specific rules relative to naming purebred dogs, and before that job is tackled, I recommend the new owner request an informational brochure on the subject from the AKC.

Permanent Registration

After the blue slip is completed and mailed to the registry with a fee, a permanent *AKC Registration Certificate* is printed and mailed to the new owner. It lists the dog's registered name, number, breed, sex, color, date of birth, sire, dam, breeder, and current owner.

If an AKC-registered dog changes ownership, a record of transfer is completed on the back of the registration certificate. The form is sent to the registry with a fee, and the new owner's name is imprinted on a new certificate.

Co-ownership of purebred dogs is possible. Those arrangements often complicate the registration process, and should be avoided whenever possible.

Stud Book Register

The Stud Book Register is a list of dogs that have produced or sired a litter that is registered with the AKC. When a bitch's or sire's first litter is registered, a date is assigned and included in all references to those animals. It appears in parentheses following the animals' registered name and number.

Pedigrees

A pedigree is a family tree. It may contain three or four generations of a registered dog's ancestry. Pedigrees are often prepared by breeders on blank forms, or on computer formats. They are not official documents in any sense of the word.

If an official AKC pedigree is desired, it can be purchased from the registry for a fee. Those documents list AKC exhibition titles as well as names and registration numbers for either 14 (three generation) or 30 (four generation) immediate ancestors of the dog. They

Health charts, pedigree, and puppy registration accompany puppies to new homes.

can also be designed to show coat colors of those ancestors.

Titles

How many times have you heard someone say, my neighbor has a grand champion thoroughbred Australian Pitbull, African Lion Dog, or some other imaginative name and title?

Just for the record, there are a number of titles that are assigned to winners of competitive events sanctioned by the AKC. The methods of assigning points and wins required to receive titles are beyond the scope of this book.

Conformation exhibitions or "dog shows" judge individuals of the same breed, and points are awarded for specific types of wins. Judges compare the animals against the breed standard that describes a perfect specimen of the breed. The title awarded to an animal that has proven its merit by earning sufficient points according to AKC rules is a *Champion of Record.* That title is abbreviated *Ch.* and is added as a prefix to a dog's name.

Field Trial competitions demonstrate the individual dog's competency in performing the functions for which it was bred. The titles awarded are *Field Champion* and *Amateur Field Champion.*

Hunting Test winners may be awarded titles of *Junior Hunter, Senior Hunter*, and *Master Hunter.*

There are three Obedience Trial classes; awards made are *Companion Dog (CD)* in the novice class, *Companion Dog Excellent (CDX)* in the open class, and *Utility Dog (UD)* in the utility class. Those titles become a suffix to the dog's name and are listed as such in registration and pedigrees.

Tracking Tests test dogs' abilities to follow trails by scent. Titles awarded include *Tracking Dog (TD),* or *Tracking Dog Excellent (TDX)* for more advanced work.

Before venturing into purebred dog registration, I heartily recommend that you acquire a copy of a general information brochure from the AKC or whatever registry you plan to use. Registration rules and regulations are not terribly complex but they differ from registry to registry, and compliance is critical.

References

Bowen, et al. 1970. Efficacy and Toxicity of Estrogens Commonly Used to Terminate Canine Pregnancy. *J.A.V.M.A.,* 186: 783–788.

Concannon, Patrick 1993. Reproductive Physiology of the Bitch. *Proceedings of Canine Theriogenology Short Course.*

Concannon, Patrick W. 1986. Canine Pregnancy and Parturition. *Veterinary Clinics of North America,* Vol. 16, No. 3: 453–473.

Johnston, Shirley D. 1995. Infertility In the Bitch. *Current Veterinary Therapy XI.*

Johnston, Shirley D. 1993. Progesterone Testing and Breeding Management in the Bitch. *Proceeding of Canine Theriogenology Short Course.*

Johnston, Shirley 1987. Clinical Manifestations of Fetal Loss in the Dog and Cat. *Veterinary Clinics of North America,* Vol. 17, No. 3: 535–551.

Kitchell, Barbara E. Mammary Tumors. *Current Veterinary Therapy XI.*

Meyers-Wallen 1993. Mismating Options. *Proceedings of Canine Theriogenology Short Course.*

Purswell, Beverly J. 1993. Diagnostic Approach to Infertility in the Bitch. *Proceedings of Canine Theriogenology Short Course.*

Sokoloweski, James 1977. Reproductive Patterns in the Bitch. *Veterinary Clinics of No. America,* Vol. 7, No. 4: 653–665.

Sokoloweski, et al., 1970. Seasonal Incidence of Estrus and Interestrous Interval for Bitches of seven breeds. *J.A.V.M.A.,* 171: 271–273.

Stubbs, W. Preston 1993. Early Neutering in the Dog and Cat. *Proceedings of Canine Theriogenology Short Course.*

Glossary

Achondrodysplasia: Congenital disease of cartilage and long bones that produces a form of dwarfism.

Ambient temperature: Surrounding environmental temperature.

Anasarca: Generalized edema of the body's connective tissues.

Anemia: Reduced quantity of red blood cells.

Anestrus: Fourth, quiet stage of the female estrous cycle.

Antibiotic: Chemical used to kill or interrupt reproduction of bacteria.

Atresia: Absence of normal opening.

Biologic: Biological product, such as a vaccine used in medicine.

Biological: Relating to life or the living process.

Bitch: Female dog, either intact or spayed.

Castration: Surgical removal of both of a male's testicles.

Cervix: Constricted opening of the female's uterus into the vagina.

Cesarean: Surgical delivery of offspring through an abdominal incision.

Colostrum: Milk containing high levels of protein and antibodies that is secreted for a few days following parturition.

Congenital: Describing a condition present at birth.

Corpus luteum: Small, white scars, formerly ovarian follicles, from which ova have been released.

Craniomandibular osteopathy: Bone disease involving the skull and lower jaw joint.

Cryptorchid: Condition in which both testicles are retained in the abdomen or inguinal canal.

Dehydration: State of body fluid deficit.

Diagnosis: Specific cause of a disease.

Diestrus: Third stage of canine estrous cycle that includes pregnancy.

Dysplasia: An abnormality of development, often referring to joints, but may be applied to soft tissue structures.

Dystocia: Difficult or prolonged birth.

Edema: Soft tissue swelling caused by a collection of plasma fluids between tissue cells.

Electrolyte solution: Solution containing various essential mineral ions.

ELISA: Enzyme-Linked ImmunoSorbent Assay, a blood analysis test technique used to determine serum hormone levels.

Embryo: Early developmental stage of an unborn animal.

Endocrine: Class of organs or glands that produce hormones.

Estrogen: Female sex hormone.

Estrous cycle: Endocrine and generative changes that take place in a female from the beginning of one estrus period to the beginning of the next.

Estrus: Canine heat period during which a female will accept a male, ovulate, and conceive.

Euthanasia: Professional, painless act of ending an animal's life for humane reasons.

Evisceration: Portions of intestine protruding from an abdominal wound.

Extended semen: Product containing fresh sperm, to which nutrients and stabilizers have been added to allow the semen to be safely chilled or frozen for storage and shipment.

Fallopian tube: One of a pair of tubes leading from the ovary to the uterine horn, also called oviduct.

Fertilization: Union of a sperm with an ovum.

Fetus: Second stage of an unborn animal, usually after about two or three weeks gestation.

Follicle: Small ovarian depression in which ova (eggs) develop.

Frenulum: Connecting fold of membrane that acts as support for a body part.

FSH: Follicle Stimulating Hormone, a hormone that originates in the pituitary gland and has its primary effect on the ovaries.

Gamete: Male or female germ cell; sperm or ovum.

Genitalia: Reproductive organs of males or females.

Gravid: Containing one or more fetuses; pregnant.

Hematocrit: Percentage of packed red blood cells in the whole blood; used to determine anemia and dehydration.

Hemorrhage: Loss of blood.

Hernia: Protrusion of an organ or tissue through an unnatural opening in the body.

Hormone: Secretory product originating from certain body cells, inciting a specific effect on other cells.

Hymen: Membrane that partially or totally occludes the external opening into the vagina from the vulva.

Hypothermia: Having a body temperature below normal.

Interestrous period: Interval between estrus periods.

Intramuscular: Injected into the muscle.

Intranasal: Administered into the nostrils by spray.

Intravenous: Injected into veins.

Intromission: Insertion of the penis into the vagina during copulation.

Kcal or kilocalorie: Also known as large calorie; amount of heat energy required to raise 1 kilogram of water from 15 to 16°C; equivalent to 1,000 calories.

Lactation: Normal milk production.

Laparoscope: Fiber optic instrument that is introduced into the abdomen through a very small incision.

Laparoscopy: Visual examination conducted by means of a laparoscope.

LH: Lutenizing hormone, a hormone originating from the pituitary gland that acts primarily on the ovarian follicles.

Malignant: Uncontrolled growth, usually relating to tumors.

Mastectomy: Surgical removal of mammary gland.

Meconium: Dark greenish feces that accumulate in the bowel of fetuses and passes from the bowel shortly after birth.

Metritis: Uterine inflammation.

Microorganisms: Organisms of microscopic or submicroscopic size, such as bacteria and viruses.

Monestrous: Experiencing one estrus period each season.

Monorchid: Condition in which one testicle is retained in the abdomen and the other is descended normally into the scrotum.

Mucous membranes: Tissue rich in mucous glands lining body passages that communicate with the exterior, such as the mouth, nasal cavity, and conjunctiva.

Neonatal: Newborn or infant.

Obese: Containing excessive quantities of body fat.

Ophthalmic: Pertaining to the eyes.

Osteopathy: Any bone disease.

Ovariohysterectomy: Surgical removal of ovaries and uterus.

Ovary: Female's paired abdominal organs that produce ova (eggs) and reproductive hormones.

Oviduct: Tubes leading from the ovaries to the uterine horns (fallopian tubes).

Ovulation: Process whereby ova are released from the ovarian follicles into the oviducts.

Ovum: Egg, or the female haploid reproductive cell; the plural is ova.

Palpation: Examining by touch.

Parturition: Process of giving birth to offspring.

Pheromone: Chemical produced by animals that stimulates a behavioral response in another of the same species.

Perineum: Body area extending from the anus downward, including external genital openings.

Pituitary gland (hypophysis): Small gland located at the base of the brain that produces many different hormones.

Placenta: Sack-like organ that envelops a fetus and attaches to the lining of the uterus, providing nutrition to unborn puppies.

Postparturient: Occurring shortly after whelping.

Proestrus: First stage of the estrous cycle manifested by vaginal bleeding.

Progesterone: Female sex hormone originating first from the corpus luteum, later from the placenta.

Prostate: One of several secondary sex glands that produce the fluid portion of the male ejaculate.

Pseudocyesis: Outward signs of pregnancy without producing an offspring; false pregnancy.

Puberty: Age at which an animal becomes capable of sexually reproducing.

Purebred: Progeny of parents of the same registered breed.

Resorption: Breaking down and assimilating embryos or fetuses without outward, visible signs of illness.

RIA: Radioimmunoassay, a blood analysis test technique used to determine serum hormone levels.

Ringer's solution: Electrolytic solution containing sodium chloride, potassium chloride, and calcium chloride in specific concentrations.

Salpingectomy: Procedure in which the fallopian tubes (oviduct) are tied or severed.

Semen: Composite ejaculate of a male, containing sperm and fluids.

Spay: Surgical removal of the ovaries and uterus; Ovariohysterectomy.

Sperm: Mobile, male reproductive cells that originate in the testicle.

Subaortic stenosis: Narrowing or constricting of vessels immediately outside the heart.

Subcutaneous: Injected under the skin.

Toxemia: Abnormal, diseased state caused by toxins or poisons in the blood.

Toxic: Poisonous; referring to a poison or toxin that may be chemical, bacterial, or metabolic in origin.

Ultrasound: Diagnostic image production by sound waves passed through the body.

Uterus: Female's hollow reproductive organ consisting of a body and two horns in which embryos are attached.

Vaccine: Man-made antigenic product designed to elicit immune response when introduced into the body.

Vagina: Hollow female reproductive organ situated between the vulva and the cervix; vaginal vault.

Vasectomy: Tying or severing of a male's vas deferens.

Vulva: Outermost female reproductive structure composed of two vertical lips.

Whelp: Process of giving birth to canine offspring.

X-ray: Diagnostic image production by radiation passed through the body.

Zygote: Cell formed by the union of two gametes (sperm and ovum); recognizable beginning of an embryo.

Index

176

177